I0540465

Memories

Memories

STORIES OF A
COUNTRY CHILDHOOD

Kirk Blackard

Memories © copyright 2025 by Kirk Blackard. All rights reserved. No part of this book may be reproduced in any form whatsoever, by photography or xerography or by any other means, by broadcast or transmission, by translation into any kind of language, nor by recording electronically or otherwise, without permission in writing from the author, except by a reviewer, who may quote brief passages in critical articles or reviews.

This book was created entirely by human authors without the use of generative AI. No part of this publication may be used in the development, training, or enhancement of artificial intelligence systems without the express written permission of the publisher.

Kirk Blackard
Houston, Texas

ISBNs: 979-8-218-72300-2

Front cover art/photo courtesy of Drew Blackard
Cover and book design by Mayfly book design

Library of Congress Catalog Number: 2025913518
First Printing: 2025

Contents

In Memory

DOUG
1943–2022

Introduction

This book is a bunch of stories about events that happened between a time a few years before I was born to a time when I was in about the seventh grade. The first two chapters tell a little about my "family of origin," that refers to my parents, siblings, and other relatives who played an important role in shaping my early experiences and development and is the foundation for who I became.

People in my family of origin came from five different actual biological families: William Radford Blackard, Eva Porter Blackard, Felix Jones, Ethel Mayfield Jones, and after Ethel's death, Ruth Cato Jones.

I never knew my grandmother Ethel Mayfield Jones or my grandfather William Redford Blackard, as both of them died before I was born. What I know about them is from stories passed down from other members of our family. I also learned about things that happened after I was born but when I was too young to remember them by listening to people who were there, mainly my parents, but also my grandparents, uncles, and aunts. For later events, which is most of the book, I have called on my memory of my own experiences and observations.

While my memory certainly is not always perfect, it's good enough for me to say with great confidence that the stories that follow accurately reflect events as they happened. Where I do not specifically remember the particulars of things that were done and said, I have inserted details and dialogue that are consistent with my recollection of what would have happened or been said.

Enjoy.

Mom and Dad

My granddad, William Radford Blackard, was born on October 5, 1867, only two years after the assassination of President Lincoln. He lived his early years in Potts Camp, Mississippi. Will later moved to Titus County, Texas, where he married Eva Lillian Porter, my Grandma Blackard, whose family had moved to Texas from North Carolina.

Dad's brother Roy, Dad, and his sister Carrie

My dad was born on July 19, 1906, the fourth of Will and Eva's eleven children. They all grew up on the family farm in Oak Grove, a very small farming community just north of Mount Pleasant. He attended elementary classes at the Oak Grove country school—two rooms, two teachers, too many bare feet and snotty noses. Dad, with a grin on his face, was known to say, "Do you know why they put buttons on the cuffs of men's coats? You don't? It's to keep guys from wiping their snotty noses on them." Dad graduated from high school—the eleventh grade—in Mt. Pleasant.

Dad attended college on and off from 1923 to 1929 at East Texas State Teachers College in Commerce, about fifty miles from Mt. Pleasant. He taught his first school before college graduation, in 1926–27 at age twenty, in the Mid-Way school, another small country school about three miles north of Oak Grove. His father and sister, Hollis, also taught there. Dad taught the 1928–29 school year at Forest Grove, another small community in Titus County.

He transferred to Sam Houston State Teachers College in Huntsville in the fall of 1929 to pursue a teacher certificate, and received his degree the following spring.

After graduation in 1930, Dad landed a job in the town of Talco, teaching agriculture and several other subjects. These were hard times. The great depres-

Oak Grove School, 1914, when Dad was eight years old
(He is at 7:30, second rwow, fourth from left.)

sion was still hanging on, banks everywhere were closed, and one of every four potential workers was unemployed. Many of Dad's friends and relatives were trying to scratch out livings plowing cotton with broken-down mules or working government jobs at very low wages. Records don't reflect Dad's earnings during his first two years of teaching, but in 1934, he earned $125 per month, which probably made him one of the higher-paid people in the area.

Talco is a small village about sixteen miles from Mt. Pleasant in Titus County. The name was taken from the initials on the wrapper of a candy bar marketed by the Texas, Arkansas, and Louisiana Candy Company. The town's population was around 350 until February, 1936, when oil was discovered, creating a boomtown

Dad as a young teacher with his class

as people flocked to the area to look for oil or to work
on the drilling rigs. They couldn't find places to sleep
or eat, but still they came, and by the late 1930s the
population was estimated at 2,000 residents, mainly
oil field workers and poor farmers and ranchers.

When the boom ended, Talco returned to normal.
It had a city hall, post office, grocery store, drug store,
dry good store, movie theatre, bank, several filling stations, and a few other small businesses when I came
to know it in the late 1940s. The school—a big brick
building housing elementary, middle, and high combined—was located on a hill about a half-mile north of
Main Street. Several churches dotted the town.

When Dad moved to Talco in 1930, he lived in
Mrs. Barton's "rooming house." He enjoyed hunting

squirrels in the woods and river bottom around Talco, and Mrs. Barton came to depend on him to put meat on the table. I can hear Dad now: "Squirrels were great. I had fun shooting them and Mrs. Barton cleaned and fried them. But I really got tired of pimento cheese sandwiches. I ate so many that I burned out on them and still can hardly stand the sight of them. Seems like all we had was those sandwiches unless I brought in squirrels. In the summer, Mrs. Barton often served watermelon about thirty minutes before supper. We thought she was trying to fill us with cheap watermelon to reduce the number of expensive pimento cheese sandwiches we ate."

Dad had a college degree, a good job, and a car. He was almost six feet tall, with a good build and wavy black hair parted down the middle. His eyes were like blue sapphires. He dated several women. And then this young lady appeared in his math class.

Mother's early life was a lot like Dad's, even though she was the daughter of a banker/rancher and Dad was the son of a schoolteacher/farmer. She lived with Granddad, Mama Ruth, and her siblings in "downtown" Talco. No one had modern conveniences or stuff like we have today, and when everyone has almost nothing, no one has much more than another. So Mother's early years were much like Dad's: outdoor toilets, drawing water from a well, heating water in a kettle to bathe in a washtub, coal oil lamps and lanterns for light, icebox to cool food, sleeping several to a room or on the porches, butchering hogs and packing the pork in chests of salt and hanging it in the smokehouse, wood-burning or coal-oil stoves, milk cow and garden to provide food.

Progress did, however, hit Talco before Oak Grove, and Mother's family obtained electricity when Mother was in grade school. In no time at all Granddad purchased an electric cook stove, a phone, and a radio. The radio was one of the few in town, and neighborhood children often gathered at the Jones's home on weekends to listen to country music and radio dramas.

Dad and Mother's romance was the talk of the town. Mother was an attractive seventeen-year-old high school student and daughter of one of the town's leading citizens. Dad was in his late twenties, was her tenth-grade math teacher, and had dated several local ladies. They started dating when Mother transferred to Mt. Pleasant for her senior (eleventh-grade) year. At first, they kept their dating a secret, but secrets don't last long in a small town like Talco. Before long, they began appearing at the soda fountain in the drugstore, attending parties around town, going to see movies in Mt. Pleasant, and doing whatever else young couples do in small towns. After graduation, Mother started college at East Texas State Teachers College in

Commerce in the fall of 1935, and they continued to see one another as often as possible.

They began talking about getting married but were worried because Mother was so young and Dad had been her teacher. One time, Dad said, "If we get married, I will probably lose my job. Don't think the school board much likes us dating and all. They will probably fire me."

Mother said "What are we going to do?"

Dad said, without hesitation, "We're gonna get married."

On Mother's eighteenth birthday, February 19, 1936, they were married by the pastor of the First Baptist Church in Commerce, in a "private ceremony," with a person who happened to be in the church building as the only witness. They spent the weekend in Dallas and returned to Talco the following Monday, where they announced their marriage to surprised family and friends. Mother's parents weren't pleased, but they accepted the marriage because of their high regard for Dad, and perhaps also because they had no other choice. Mother dropped out of college and returned to Talco.

During those oil-boom years, living space was so hard to find that the new couple moved into Mrs. Barton's rooming house, in the room where Dad had been living. After a few months, they moved to an old, deserted building on the Talco school ground with a shop at one end and a classroom at the other, which they fixed as their living quarters. They didn't have a cook stove, which didn't matter all that much since Mother couldn't cook anyway. A year or so later, Mother and Dad built a small, four-room and one bath house and furnished it with a table, chairs, bed, and coal-oil-burning stove, where they lived for several years.

After his father died in 1935, Dad helped support Grandma and the younger kids who were still at home on his salary of about $150 a month. Almost every Saturday, and frequently during the week, he drove to Oak Grove and delivered groceries and ice for their icebox. He also helped several of his younger siblings attend college, although eventually they repaid most of the money.

In 1939 my parents moved to Valley View in Cooke County, where Dad got a job teaching vocational agriculture and shop. Valley View was similar to Talco. It was a small farming village of about 700 people, a wide spot in the road between Gainesville and Dallas. It had a town square with a few surrounding streets, a two-story brick schoolhouse for grades one through twelve, five or six churches, a couple of filling stations, a laundromat, a drugstore with a snack bar, a small bank, and a general store where several old

Dad

Mother

men gathered to play dominoes just about every day except Sunday. Mother and Dad made many friends and enjoyed doing what young couples do. They went on local camping trips—Mother and a friend made a four-person tent with a divider down the middle—and occasionally traveled to the hills of Arkansas. On one occasion, they traveled to Colorado.

Then kids started coming

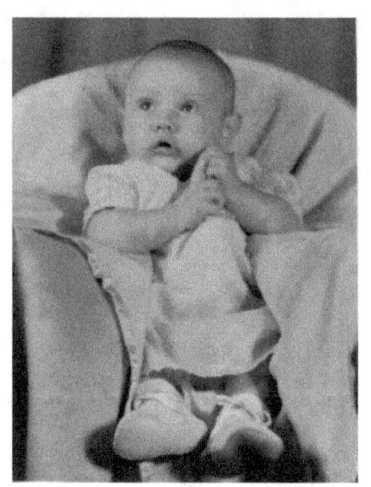

Me

Family

Dad checked Mother into a hospital in Gainesville, a town only slightly larger than Valley View and about ten miles away, on April 14, 1941. The doctor briefly examined her, walked out into the waiting room, and said, "Fred, it's gonna be a while. You may as well go get a bite to eat and prepare for the long haul." Dad walked down the street to a greasy spoon diner. When he returned after breakfast, the doctor said, "It's here. You have a son." They say I cried for the better part of the first year.

Mother and Dad were anticipating their second child in late November, 1943. They prepared a nursery, and Dad built a baby bed in the school shop. Dad went to school one morning, and about an hour later Mother called her friends, the Lathams, who found Dad and they all went to the hospital in Gainesville. Doug, Dianne, and Donna made their surprising arrival on November 30.

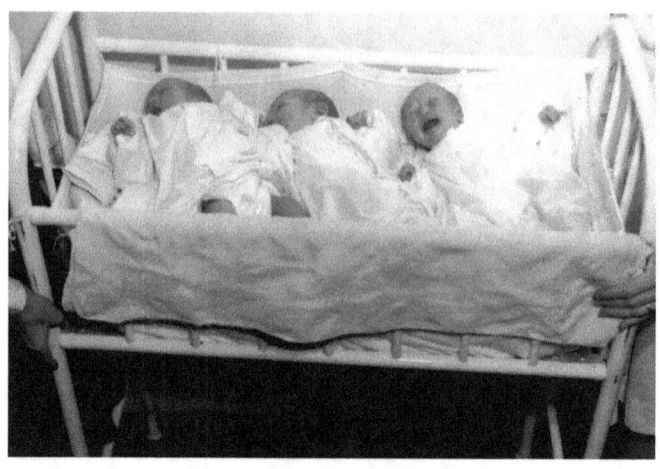

You guess

Dad called Mother's parents with the news and talked to Granddad. He suspected a trick, so he called Anna Ruth, Mother's sister, to see if she had been told the same thing. She had. When they told Mama Ruth, she almost fainted.

The triplets quickly became a local sensation. Their pictures were in several local papers. Carnation Milk Company donated condensed milk for as long as they would drink it. Another company donated baby food for a short time. Friends and strangers turned out to look and offered to help. Mama Ruth came for a week, and Anna Ruth for a second week to lend a hand with the four of us kids.

Dad returned to the shop and made two more beds. He also started looking for a larger house and found a boxy, wood-frame one with faded white siding on

The Triplets
Doug, top. Donna, left. Dianne, right.

a couple of acres out near the edge of town. It had five rooms and modern fixtures—indoor plumbing, running hot water, electric lights, a Frigidaire, and a hand-cranked telephone on a party line. With help from the Lathams and Hoffmans, Mother and Dad cleaned, painted, wallpapered, and generally made it livable. Most importantly, Dad converted one room to a nursery with a glass door to allow the endless stream of friends, acquaintances, and curious strangers to see the triplets without being in the room with them. I'm told I was a reasonable tour guide.

Can you imagine the number of yellow, brown, stinky cloth diapers a set of healthy, well-fed triplets generate? The local laundromat donated a washing machine with a wash tub and three rinse tubs, which Dad set up on the back porch. Clothes, mainly diapers, were slapped around in a tub of hot soapy water and then moved from tub to tub between two rubber rollers for rinsing. After the last squeeze, they were hung on the clothesline out in the backyard, where they flapped around in the wind until they were dry. Mother washed diapers every morning, and, on more than one occasion, young parents from the military base in Gainesville observed them on the line and stopped to ask about leaving their children at the day care center. Mother told them she already had plenty babies.

In the early days, friends from the community organized shifts and took turns bringing food, helping with the laundry, washing bottles and babies, and babysitting. Later on, Mother's special friend Ruby Jewell and a wonderful lady named Mary were mainstays. Ruby Jewell usually helped mother until noon and then took me home with her for the afternoon.

Dad's main parenting role was taking care of me. He claimed he couldn't do much with the triplets because changing stinky diapers made him throw up. Perhaps it did, as one cold day when we were traveling in the car, one of the triplets filled a diaper, and shortly after, Dad was vomiting outside one door and I outside the other. Mother was busy.

Buddies

I spent a lot of time with Dad during those years. He sat in his chair in the living room and read the paper almost every evening, and he made me a small chair so I could sit next to him and pretend to read as well. I frequently accompanied Dad as he visited local farms or took agriculture students on field trips and developed my lifelong fondness for chicken-fried steak on one of these trips. Dad loaded a couple of boys and me into his car and another five or six boys and a bunch of camping gear into a two-wheel trailer, and we struck out for some campground up in Oklahoma. Our meals were mostly baloney sandwiches that each person packed from home, but occasionally the group had café hamburgers. One time we had chicken-fried steak

Our family, circa 1945

for about three times the price. I liked it. After that, when Dad and the boys ordered hamburgers, I ordered steak. Can't recall how long he let me get by with it.

I don't remember Mother or Dad ever raising their voice with me, and the only spanking I remember occurred about this time. Mother was in town with us four kids in the car. She was visiting with her friend, Mrs. Browning, at the curb in front of Latham Grocery—no doubt a real challenge under the circumstances. I wanted to say something, and got directly to the point: "Mother, shut up. I have something to say." I don't remember what Mother said. I do remember the spanking I received when Mother told Dad what I had done.

Dad tried to do a little farming on the couple of acres where we lived at the edge of town. He usually raised a garden, sometimes adopted a couple of orphan calves, had several hens for eggs, and kept a milk cow. One time Dad was milking the cow on a hot, sweaty evening. She kicked several times, kept moving around, and continually swatted Dad in the face with her tail. Dad tried to calm her but instead got more and more worked up himself. Then that cow stepped into the milk bucket. Dad hauled off and kicked her as hard as he could and broke his toe. We didn't have much milk that day.

One afternoon, I was feeding the hens, which involved putting a small amount of grain into a little bucket, walking out into the chicken yard, and scattering handsfulls on the ground for the hens to eat. Simple enough, except that the hens were always hungry and had little patience for waiting. One day, just as I was about to throw the first handfull, the entire mob came rushing toward me like a pack of starving wildcats, clucking, scratching—threatening, as far as I could tell. I had to defend myself! I saw a part of an old car bumper that just happened to be there in the yard and picked it up to use as a weapon against those hens. I took a powerful wind-up, drew back for delivery, and—hit myself on the top of the head. Blood oozed. I cried, threw the bucket at those awful hens, and ran away as fast as I could.

I can't remember much about my first year of school, but I do remember one thing that happened. I was selected as the first-grade Halloween king. My job was to wear my best clothes and walk into a school assembly with the first-grade queen. Now walking with

The killer chickens and me

the girl was bad enough, and the collar was tight as a hatband. Feeling humiliated and choked, I registered what seemed like a mild objection. Mrs. Stinson, my old maid teacher, looked down on me, grabbed my arm, gave it a hard squeeze, and told me in her own whiny voice to cut out the whining and live up to the great honor of being king. Right there in front of the queen and everyone. I suppose I did, as I don't remember any further problems.

Queen and King

Our Move

When he was a young man during the depression years, Dad had bought some land in the Oak Grove community from family and friends who needed to sell in order to live. He had bought 65 acres from his mother and dad in 1934 for $1065, 100 acres from his sister and her husband for $3500, and 250 acres from a local family for $6,643.

In the summer of 1948, when I was seven years old, our family moved to Titus County to live on that land, with a stopover of about eight years in the Greenhill community while Mom and Dad worked to save money to build a house on the land.

That move was a turning point in my life that I could not have imagined. I was a town (admittedly a very small town) kid in Valley View. We lived on a street rather than a road. Dad had one job, teaching. Mother was a teacher's wife, not a farmer's wife. School had twelve grades. We had a phone and indoor toilets. Neighbors were close enough to see our dirty laundry.

Greenhill was different. We moved to the country and a different way of life that would provide different memories and shape our lives in different ways. I don't remember how I felt about the move, or even if I had any feelings about it.

Our move started with a buzz. Mr. Cameron, our neighbor from across a narrow gravel street, raised honey bees. Unfortunately, he picked our moving day to harvest his honey, and in the process greatly agitated those bees. As Dad and some friends hauled furniture from the house to the moving truck, mad bees attacked them with a fury. Dad and the other movers wore protective masks provided by Mr. Cameron as they carried furniture with one hand and slapped bees with the other. We kids stayed inside

We stayed with Mama Ruth and Granddad for our first several days in Titus County. The first morning we were there, Dad, Doug, and I went to check out our new house. That trip was my first real memory. What I now know about life before that is from things I have read or from what other people have told me, or from recalling a few specific things that happened from time to time, like the only spanking I ever received or running from bees that day, that don't seem to be part of where I ended up.

I remember driving to our new house as the start of a new and different life. I thought we were going through the back side of nowhere. We drove about fifteen miles from Talco, which was almost nowhere itself, on mostly rough dirt roads; over narrow, rickety board bridges; through worn out cotton fields now filled with dark and forbidding forests of sassafras, persimmon, oak, sweetgum, and pine trees.

Shortly before we arrived at our new house, we stopped at Rolf's store to meet our new neighbor and buy food for lunch. The store, and Mr. Barrett's look-alike store just across the road, were the center of the Greenhill community. Both were old, weather-beaten wood buildings with rusting tin roofs and a single hand-operated gasoline pump out front. Each one sold several kinds of food, sacks of cattle and hog feed, gasoline and motor oil, and all sorts of soda and candy for a nickel and jaw breakers, bubble gum, and other sweets for one cent each. We visited them often over the next several years to spend our weekly twenty-five cent allowance.

Dad ordered a hunk of rat cheese and some baloney. Mr. Rolf grabbed a huge kitchen knife and never stopped talking as he cut the cheese from an eighteen-inch "wheel" and the baloney from a three-foot-long tube. I guess he was talking to Doug and me, because Dad was searching the store. He grabbed two cans of sardines, a box of crackers, a big onion, three bottles of pop, and three peanut patties. We drove down the road, sat on the ground under a huge oak tree among the weeds and ticks and chiggers, and had our first meal at our new home.

Home

Greenhill had a few houses of various sizes and shapes on small farms, an elementary school with seven grades and about thirty students, the two small country stores, and three churches—Methodist, Presbyterian, and Church of Christ.

Our new (to us, really old and kind of broken-down) house, belonged to the school and was considered to be part of the pay for the school principal, which Dad was to be when school started. It was on the school ground—so close to the school building that it seemed I could almost spit from one to the other. The yard, the same for school and house, hadn't been mowed since the year before and was more a jungle than a playground. Tall weeds covered the area and there were several huge old oak trees and a half dozen big bare spots where mudholes had been in the spring. Little pyramids of dried mud that marked crawdad holes were scattered around. A couple of broken-down seesaws sat between the house and the road.

The house was really just a cabin: a kitchen, living room, and one bedroom under a dull tin roof, badly in need of paint, looking sad enough to cry. The school board had agreed to add a second bedroom, which was built later that summer. Dad built an outhouse out near the edge of the woods, so we didn't have to use the ones for the schoolkids. Mother and Dad took the original bedroom, and the four of us kids the new one. Several years later when our parents decided the girls and boys shouldn't be sleeping in the same room, Dad hired a local carpenter, and they added two more rooms and a very small back porch. We put a basketball goal on a pole about thirty feet from the porch and hung a light on an extension cord out the back door so we could play at night. Doug and I played "horse," "pig," or one-on-one, and often invited our sisters or neighbor kids and played bigger games. During wet months, the entire area became a sea of slop—worse than a pigpen.

The water supply, while it lasted, was a cistern—a big hole in the ground, perhaps twenty-five feet wide and forty feet deep, lined with bricks and mortar—that collected rainwater runoff from the roof of the school. Water was piped from it to one faucet in the kitchen. We got our hot water from a teakettle on the kitchen stove that burned butane gas from a tank out in the yard. The cistern often went dry toward the end of summer, which gave Dad a chance to clean it out. I'm not sure he ever told Mother about the dead rat he found in it one year. When the cistern went dry during hot summers, we hauled water in jars and milk cans from a nearby spring.

We bathed, when we did, in a #3 washtub on the kitchen floor. Mother mixed cold water with hot water from the teakettle, producing enough to bath in, and we four kids took turns bathing. When the last one— usually me, the oldest and presumably the dirtiest, finished, Dad carried the tub out and dumped it in the back yard.

When nature called, day or night, winter or summer, we usually walked fifty yards or so to the outhouse, although Mother did keep a two-gallon metal pot with a good lid, a "chamber pot," for us to use when the weather was really bad.

Each room had an electric light, but telephones didn't reach our part of the country until a couple of years later, when a party line shared by several households was installed. When one family was using it, the others couldn't, yet there was no privacy, as everyone could be on the line at the same time.

The six of us, along with a Cocker Spaniel named Joe—the name was Dad's idea, after Joe Barrow, Dad's brother-in-law who had given us the dog—lived in this house for about eight years until Mother and Dad were able to build a new one on the farm in Oak Grove. To build the house, they borrowed $10,400 from the Federal Land Bank, making semi-annual payments of $414.45 until the note was paid off in 1970.

Our family, circa 1949
Triplets, left to right: Dianne, Doug, Donna

Lost

Dad bought his first cow soon after moving to Greenhill. He wanted a milk cow to help feed us kids, and he bought one from a local farmer. She was about ten years old, had wide hips, narrow shoulders, and a big round, low-slung belly covered by a dull mustard-colored coat. Large, brown, saucer-like eyes protruded from each side of her head. This cow was no prize, but she gave enough milk to raise a good calf and four kids.

And that old cow was almost the end of me. I remember the day well. "Kirk . . . Kirk . . . Get up son." My sleepy brain told me Dad was waking me earlier than usual. "You need to get out of bed and give me a hand. The milk cow wasn't at the barn this morning. Don't know where she is. I have business in town, so you need to find her."

Rolling out of bed, wiping the sleep from my eyes, I pulled on a mostly white T-shirt and a pair of jeans with a small hole in each knee before stumbling into the kitchen for breakfast. Scrambled eggs, bacon, and toast were already on the table. Dad had coffee and Mother had hot tea. I had sweet milk from a jar with white liquid on the bottom and thick, yellow, jelly-like cream on top. Mother stirred the two layers, but they didn't mix. The cream just broke into small yellow pieces of butter in the white liquid. I tried to strain the stuff with my teeth. That's the way it is with raw milk, straight from the family cow.

Our new milk cow didn't have a name. We just called her "the milk cow." She came to the barn early every morning and late every afternoon. Dad milked her every morning and most afternoons. I was eight years old, so sometimes I pinch-hit for him in the afternoon, balancing on a small three-legged stool, head against the cow's flank, bucket on the ground between her legs.

Some people milked cows with one hand at a time, but I took pride in being a two-handed milker: using alternating hands, I squeezed and released the fingers of her udder to maintain a steady flow. Sometimes I directed a stream of milk into a stray cat's mouth or perhaps at one of my siblings who happened to be in the area.

Dad knew something was wrong when the cow didn't show up that morning. My job was to find her and bring her home.

I struck out walking across the dewy, soggy pasture

to the sound of "be careful" from my parents. The field was about a half-mile deep and narrow enough that I could see both sides from the middle. The part nearest to our house was generally open, although spotted with occasional scrub cedar trees, small bushy oaks, bunches of persimmon trees, and patches of wild dewberries.

Try as I might, I couldn't find that cow in the open front part of the pasture. My only choice was to explore the wooded area further from home, an area I had never visited. The back third of the property was heavily wooded with huge oak, hickory, black jack, and pine trees, intermingled with wild grape, sumac, and other bushes. The late spring leaves shaded the light of the sun and created a dim, shadowy world in which I could see only a few yards. Everything looked the same in all directions. No surprise that although Doug and I had been to the small pond at the edge of the trees to fish for perch and try to shoot frogs with our Red Ryder BB guns, we had never dared to go further into the forest.

My venture into the woods seemed surprisingly easy at first. The shade of the trees provided relief from the now blazing sun. There was no path, but zigzagging around the trees and bushes was not a problem. I walked slowly along, trying to call her by yelling "Mooooo-cow" from time to time. Presently, I arrived at the rusty, old, barbed wire fence at the back of the pasture. There she stood—on the other side, staring intently at me with her bright, round eyes. I decided to break a hole in the fence, get my rope around her neck, and lead her through the hole to the barn.

I pushed one of the rotten posts over, stood on it for a minute, a wire popped, and we were ready to go. But getting my rope on that cow was another matter. Holding her cocky head high, she looked directly at me and let me approach within a few feet. I almost got my rope around her neck and she ran away—not far, just enough to make me start over again. After many repetitions of that silly game, I was frustrated, impatient, and hotter than a firecracker. I choked back tears of anger. Finally, the cow had enough as well, and she darted through the hole in the fence and ran off into the woods, out of sight. I was alone.

I couldn't decide whether to chase her or give up and head for home. Without really deciding on either course, I started walking, winding my way around the trees and bushes in whatever direction was easiest.

Suddenly, I didn't know where I was, where I was going, or how to get there. The less I knew, the faster I ran. I panicked and beat it through the wilderness. No longer picking easy routes, I charged through thickets of bushes and briars. Sweat streamed down my face from the heat of the day and the exertion, but mostly from the fear.

A clearing appeared, and I relaxed. This no doubt was the open meadow of the front pasture, and just beyond it was home. My scary adventure was almost over, or so I thought.

Before long I realized that the clearing was not our familiar pasture. It was only a small opening in the forest, and dead ahead was a swamp the likes of which I had never seen. I continued my frantic run straight into the swamp, as though there was reason to believe this was the right direction. Grass and weeds were thick and waist high. Stinky, dark water stood in puddles at every turn. My feet grew wet and heavy from the caked mud. Mosquitoes and stinging flies hit me from every direction. Bushes and briars scraped and pricked me. I could see only a few feet ahead. I had to zigzag continually to make any progress. Mostly I worried about what I couldn't see: mushy quicksand with no bottom, where a person could sink all the way to China, never to be seen again. Water moccasin snakes with their deadly venom. All the other critters looming in this forbidding place.

Just as I began to wonder if that swamp would never end, the familiar trees of the forest appeared ahead. Greatly relieved, I made my way toward what I hoped to be the other side of the woods, content at least that the worst was behind me.

Wrong! My heart sank as if it had fallen into the dreaded quicksand. Then it began to race with fear. In front of me was another swamp just like the first. Would this never end? I charged blindly through it, not realizing until much later that I had been running in circles and was in the very same swamp again. Getting through it from a new direction was no less difficult or scary, however.

Finally, I reached the other side. Still lost, I continued walking. I was running out of gas and moving at a rather slow pace, but I was out of the dreaded swamps at last.

In the distance, I saw telephone poles and power lines—signs of a familiar road I could follow home. Relieved, excited, and bone-tired, I ran through the high grass toward the road and home.

Wrong again! Instead of the familiar road I came upon an unfamiliar railroad—just two parallel ribbons of steel piercing the horizon in opposite directions with no landmarks to guide me. My heart hit bottom. I still had no idea where I was or which way to go. One minute I thought I was almost home, the next more lost than ever. Exhausted, hurting, and scared, I didn't know anything to do except keep walking.

Home appeared suddenly. I rushed ahead toward the house, sobbing with relief. Dad had returned from town, and my parents were about to begin looking for me. Instead, they welcomed me home. I doubt that they were as happy to see me as I was to see them.

The cow had arrived home hours earlier. After she jumped through the hole in the fence, she went straight to the barn, while I wandered around for hours, directionless, in the dark wilderness and hostile swamp. I think the lesson of all this is that we all need to know where we are and where we are going if we expect to get there. Otherwise, even a cow might beat us.

Church

We attended church as a family for many years, driving to Talco every Sunday and worshipping at the Talco Church of Christ with several members of Mother's family. When we moved to our house on the farm, Dad went his own way and attended the Nevil's Chapel Baptist Church. We kids went to the Oak Grove Church of Christ with our mother.

We were in church every Sunday morning unless we were sick, and on most Sunday and Wednesday evenings. Excuses for missing were hard to come by. We usually attended vacation Bible school for a week in early summer and a week-long gospel meeting in July or August.

One year—I'm guessing after the second or third grade—we went to Bible school at the Greenhill Presbyterian Church. The church was founded in 1860 and, from what I could see, the building was constructed about the same time. It was a large wood structure with high ceilings, a high-pitched roof, a small front

Sunday best

porch, peeling white paint, and ceiling fans rather than air conditioning. The building was one large room with a classroom in each corner. The outside walls were filled with large windows that were raised to let the air in during the hot Texas summers.

Our last event of the day was held in one of the small classrooms at the front of the building. When the teacher dismissed class, all the boys jumped out of one of the big windows. Except for me. I walked out the classroom door, through the sanctuary, and out the front door. No doubt like a perfect little gentleman.

Mother was waiting in the car and saw it all. When I climbed in, she said, "I can't believe those boys had the nerve to jump out the church window. I'm really glad you aren't like them. If you had done that, I wouldn't have allowed you to come back. I'm proud of you."

Oak Grove Church of Christ

The truth is, I was at the head of the line to jump out that window when I remembered that my new straw hat was in the sanctuary. By the time I found it, the fastest way out was through the front door, so that's the way I went. I never did tell Mother. Somehow, I think God has forgiven me for what I intended to do and for what I didn't do that day.

School

We had hardly settled in from the move to the country when school started. I entered second grade at Greenhill along with thirty-five kids in grades one through seven. Mrs. Justice, a nice lady in her mid-forties, with long dark hair usually fashioned in a bun on top, bright red dresses, and reading glasses hanging on a string around her neck, was the teacher for grades one through three. Dad was principal, fourth–seventh grade teacher, coach, custodian, counselor, librarian, hall monitor, security officer, and bell ringer.

When Dad rang the bell—a real, old-fashioned bell with a six-inch handle and clapper—on that first day, all the kids from fourth through seventh grade ran to the front door and lined up outside by grade, ready to march in upon command. The first through third grade kids formed a similar formation at the back door—except for one. I didn't realize I was in the wrong line 'til the big kids started teasing me. Dad sent me to the back door, embarrassed as I could be, and I sneaked quietly to the end of the second-grade line. When Mrs. Justice gave the command, we all marched in and took our seats. The very next day, Dad did away with that march in.

The schoolhouse was a wood-frame building, painted white but peeling badly, as sad looking as our house. It had four large rooms, two on each side of a wide hall, a green, high-pitched roof, and huge windows. A small library near the front held books from bygone times. During my first several years, two of the rooms were used as classrooms, one as a place for all sorts of junk, and one as a playroom during bad weather. During my later years, the junk room was converted to a cafeteria that served lunch.

Two, two-hole outhouses were about sixty yards away; one for the girls near the woods on one side of the schoolyard and the one for the boys on the other side.

The "little room" for grades one through three had three rows of desks and a few tables scattered about, and the "big room" for grades four through seven had four rows of desks, with those in each row slightly larger than in the previous one. All the rooms had high ceilings and cracks through the floor. The building was on piers, and, during winter, cold air rushed in through the cracks and some days the rooms felt like a refrigerator. On these days, we had class ganged around the

Greenhill school building with extended family members
Top row: Kirk, Cousin Janell, Uncle Cato
Middle row: Uncle Virgil and Doug, Donna, Dianne
Bottom row: Cousins Phil, Lana, Charles

big space heater in the corner, much like a group of chicks crowding around a mother hen for warmth.

Quite often, Dad conducted a spelling bee or arithmetic contest on Friday afternoons. In a spelling bee, two captains were selected, and they chose the kids for their sides. Dad lined us up—a team in a row on each side of the room—and went down the lines calling words to be spelled. When someone missed, they sat down. Last team with someone standing won. Arithmetic contests were one-on-one tests of speed and accuracy, starting with the little kids. One student from each team went to the chalkboard, Dad gave them a problem, and the first to solve it won. The winner took on the next person from the other team, and the last team with someone standing won. If we did well, sometimes Dad dismissed school a few minutes early.

I don't remember any behavior problems. Paddling was officially okay, but Dad almost never used it. I think he convinced kids he would, and that was all it took. There was an occasional fight, and sometimes I was involved. Larry, Peatie, Earl, and Clyde were good friends, but from time to time we had a disagreement. Maybe sometimes they wanted to whip the teacher's kid, or they had bad attitudes, or I had a bad attitude, or we were just boys being boys. Who knows. In any case, when we had disagreements, we resolved them in our own way, as recess was often not well- monitored and during afternoon PTA meetings there was no supervision at all.

One of my fights occurred during our lunch period, sixth grade. Dad, my siblings, and I went home to eat, as there was no cafeteria at the time and home was only a few yards away. Mother asked me to ride my bike to Rolf's store to get a loaf of bread. I guess a problem had been brewing because I was involved in a fight before I rode out of sight. Dad watched the whole thing and didn't do anything. He told me later that he expected me to handle my own problems, and if I got involved in a fight, I needed to finish it.

I don't remember many kids failing, and most of us did pretty well when we advanced to town school. I'll never understand how Dad and Mrs. Justice did it, teaching three or four grades in one room. The only help they had was Mrs. White, an assistant who visited each of the country schools every couple of weeks to help with teaching chores and deliver library books—I preferred the biographies with orange covers. Each teacher taught one grade, usually three or four students at a time, while kids in the other grades did assignments, helped one another, listened to another class, or just faked it.

Christmas at School

Christmas was a special time at school. A few days before the holiday recess the entire student body rambled through the nearby fields to capture the perfect Christmas tree. Dad dismissed classes early, grabbed an ax, and struck out across the pasture near the school, with kids following close behind. We were a rowdy bunch of grade school kids in high anticipation of the approaching holidays.

The field was spotted with cedar trees of various sizes and shapes. None really seemed as pretty as a store-bought tree, but all were green and would hold ornaments. Every tree was best from some kid's point of view. I don't remember how we decided on the right one, but, somehow, a decision was made and the one with the best size and shape available was selected. Dad chopped it down with his ax. Then Peatie, Clyde, Suzy, Earl, Sandra, Patricia, and a host of other kids surrounded the tree—big kids up front at the heavy end and little ones to the back—and carried it slowly across the pasture to the school. Everyone then joined in applying the decorations—worn-out colored balls, strings made from paper or popcorn, new store-bought icicles, a foil star on top. Can't imagine what it looked like. We thought it was beautiful.

The highlight of the Christmas season at school was the Christmas plays. The "little room" presented one performance and the "big room" another. As soon as school started on the last day before the holidays, Dad gathered all the biggest boys and raised the wall between the two schoolrooms. Yes, raised the wall. The wall separating the two was actually made that way—the bottom part was movable, so it could be raised into the top half like you were raising a gigantic wooden window, creating one big room. "Ready, set, one, two, three, lift!" Everyone grunted and groaned together, and gradually two rooms became one bigger room. We then rearranged the chairs and held the performance on one side of the double-sized room.

The combined classes sang Christmas songs under Mrs. Justice's direction. I was often assigned to ring Christmas bells. This meant standing in the center back row and shaking a handful of bells like I had ants in my pants. At the time, I thought the assignment was an honor. I now suspect Mrs. Justice assigned the bells to me because I couldn't carry a tune, and she thought that ringing the bells would prevent me from singing loud enough to mess up the songs more than they already were.

The Christmas play of my seventh-grade year was about a kid, close to my age, who ate too much for Christmas dinner and got sick to his stomach. The leading character in the play was the kid's father, and Dad offered this part to Larry or me, as we were the oldest boys in school, and at least in theory closest to the father's age. Larry and I both turned the lead down! We never talked about it, and I don't know why Larry made the decision he did. Dad probably wondered why I turned him down. The truth is that I read the script, and the script said the father kissed the mother, and that was way, way too much for me to handle. Imagine kissing a girl in front of about a hundred people! No way.

When I rejected the father role, Dad assigned me to play the kid with the stomachcache. It turns out that I had recently had an operation on my arm, so my arm had a large bandage on it, which the mothers and fathers in attendance had never seen. They thought it was a prop for the play and never did understand how eating too much had hurt my arm.

The rest of the story is that Dad assigned the biggest girl in the school to play the father. She/he never did kiss the wife. And the parents were greatly confused—with a girl playing the father and a boy with an arm bandaged because he ate too much Christmas dinner.

4-H Club

The school didn't have the clubs and other activities that are offered today. The only one I can remember was the 4-H club, a national organization for farm boys and girls. About once a month, the local county agriculture agent showed up to conduct a meeting of some sort—just what we did escapes me. I do remember, however, that we did club "yells," and the agent said Greenhill kids were the best—perhaps he said loudest—yellers in the county.

The organization had a "borrow a pig" program through which kids could receive a free female pig, raise the pig, raise a litter of its pigs, and give one of them to another kid. I got a young pig from another kid and fed it every day and took care of it and then took care of the nine pigs in her litter. My expenses were pretty low because Dad let me use his pig feed. When the pigs weighed about a hundred pounds each, I gave one to another kid and sold the whole remaining bunch for enough to buy a couple of cows.

Participation in the 4-H club provided my first opportunity to take a trip away from home. During the summer after my sixth grade, I was selected as one of four students from various schools to represent the county at the state 4-H convention at A&M. I only remember two things about it. One is that we drove there in the county agent's un-air-conditioned car (no one had air-conditioned cars), and he was a big smoker, and I sat in the seat behind him and breathed his smoke for the entire trip. Maybe that experience is one reason I never smoked.

The other memory is much more pleasant. I thought the girl from Chapel Hill was just about the prettiest girl I had ever seen. She had a pretty face, smooth complexion, and long blond hair. She was older than me—just enough to make her exciting.

Sports

Sports were important at Greenhill, as well as the other schools in the county. We played them mainly at recess and sometimes for a few minutes after school, before kids started for home. There were rarely enough kids to field both boy and girl teams, particularly in softball, and quite often several girls were better players than many of the boys, so they played on the school team.

Softball season was in fall and spring. Our diamond was located in the area of the school ground that had the most grass with the fewest trees and mudholes. We used burlap bags filled with sand for bases. Base paths were the natural trails that eventually wore in the grass from repeated use—much like cow paths. Our backstop was usually okay, but sometimes it was small and full of holes, and sometimes there was none at all. We often spent a lot of time chasing balls that had gone over, around, or through the backstop, if there was one.

We played "scrub" most of the time, with anywhere from six or eight kids to the entire student body. Field

positions were filled and everybody else rotated bat-
ting until they were out, in which case they went to the
field and replaced the next person in line to become a
batter. Sometimes we chose sides and actually played
games. Dad refereed some games, but mostly the biggest, meanest kid at school made the close calls. We
spent almost as much time chasing balls and arguing
close calls as we did pitching and catching.

Occasionally our team played another of the country
schools—Nevil's Chapel, Oak Grove, Mid-Way, Chapel
Hill, Argo, Union Grove, Bridges Chapel, or another
school long since gone and forgotten. On game day,
many of us came to school early for a quick practice,
and we usually couldn't concentrate on our studies.
We got out of school early and sometimes traveled a
few miles to a neighboring school. Everybody got to
use a glove, as the two teams shared gloves until all the
fielders had one. The game had umpires—one of the
teachers—to cut down on the arguments and fighting.
We had extra balls, so we could play while someone
else chased errant ones. We had a winner and a loser,
and occasionally bragging rights.

Basketball season was during winter, except when
the weather was too cold to be outside. We didn't
have uniforms, and even if we had, it was often too
cold to wear such skimpy attire. Coats were better.
Our basketball court was a flat area of grass and dirt

Greenhill softball team

just north of the softball diamond. It had homemade backboards and baskets, more or less ten feet high, placed more or less ninety feet apart. The court lines were scratches—sometimes straight but more often crooked—drawn in the ground with a garden hoe or the heel of someone's shoe.

The court surface was a particular problem when we played Oak Grove, a school that was located in a very sandy area of the county. The boundary lines drawn in the sand disappeared as soon as the game was underway, and trying to dribble the ball in the deep sand was almost impossible. Play continued as long as the players were more or less between the two goals, and the teachers officiating the game made allowances for traveling caused by ground conditions.

My uncle, Joe Barrow, was the teacher and coach at Oak Grove. Uncle Joe and Dad had a gentlemanly but very real rivalry when it came to sports. Each of them went to extra lengths to beat the other. We sometimes wondered if Uncle Joe put his court on the sandiest, softest place available and then taught his kids how to take advantage of the sand. Probably he didn't. But every time he beat us we wondered about it.

Playing basketball with girls had its own special challenges. I remember this big ol' girl on the Mid-Way team. She wasn't all that pretty—a rather plain face, hair in bad need of attention, a little overweight. But she moved like a duck on a June bug, was tough as a chicken gizzard, and could shoot like the basket was a barn door. We played Mid-Way several times during my career, and Dad always assigned me to guard her. During the first game, I was guarding her a little too close, and the referee (who just happened to be the Mid-Way teacher) whistled a foul and announced to the world that I was guilty of "hugging." My face got even redder, my sweat even heavier, as I watched her sink her free throws. After that, I made sure to stay far enough away from her to avoid being accused of hugging.

The highlights of the seasons in softball and basketball were the County Meets, when all the little country schools gathered in Mt. Pleasant for a tournament. County Meet had real officials in real uniforms, and the winners received a real trophy. Softball had a backstop and real bases. Basketball was played in a gymnasium. This was the first inside game of the year for most of us, and going to County Meet in town was a big deal. We sat in the stands and watched other teams play while waiting for our games. We visited a concession stand for popcorn and soda water. Sometimes we had lunch at the Dairy Queen.

Track season was one day a year—the day of the track County Meet. Dad just packed us all up, took us to the track, assigned us to events, and gave us some good coaching. He said, "Never look back. Someone may be gaining on you." And "Never give up because you are hurting. The other guy is probably hurting more than you are." I don't remember us winning many races. I think speed also had something to do with it.

Marbles was our off-season sport, played mostly in the spring after basketball and before softball, or just about any time after class. At Greenhill, we had two games. One was a little like golf. Some kid with a pocketknife would dig a series of small holes in the ground. Players took turns shooting their marbles from hole to hole—shoot 'till you miss, then lose your turn. The first player to hit all the holes out and back was the winner. The other game involved placing marbles on a line or in a circle and then using a "taw" marble to shoot them off the line or out of the circle.

Marbles were often used as playground currency. A large or small one traded for several regular ones. A clear agate was best and often traded for quite a few regular marbles. Sometimes marbles were traded for gum, candy, or a stale egg sandwich, but they were rarely traded for money because so few kids had any.

First Work

School provided my first opportunity to work for a wage and, to a very small extent, go into business for myself. The wage wasn't much, but it was a job, in second grade.

One of Dad's daily tasks was to sweep the classrooms, and early in that first year he had me sweep the "little" room for ten cents a day. I remember going through the motions every afternoon after class, trying to push as much dirt and other crud in the same direction as possible. I stuck with it until I graduated from the seventh grade.

Every day was payday for the first week, and, after that, Dad paid me once at the end of the school year. At the end of that first year, he gave me a small calf instead of the money. We followed the same procedure every year, and, with money from the 4-H club's "borrow a pig" program, I began to accumulate a small herd that was intended to help pay for my college. I suppose it did, in an indirect way. By the time I started college,

I had a herd of ten or twelve cows. Dad and I never discussed me selling them or who would pay my college expenses. I was awarded a small scholarship, and he gave me a checkbook and told me to write checks on him for any additional money I needed. I didn't abuse the trust, and he never took the offer back. After graduation from college, I told him I did not intend to sell my cows, and he should consider them as part of his herd, which they sorta had been all along. I figure I got the better of the deal.

Bare Feet, Burrs, and Bull Nettles

We kids usually began shedding our shoes as early as possible each year. The first barefoot day was a rite of passage from winter, through spring, directly into summer. The weather determined exactly when the event occurred, but like moths emerging from cocoons, bare feet began to appear in the schools and on the playgrounds around April Fools' Day each year. We Blackard children were fortunate to go barefoot only for fun when the desire hit us, but some of our friends did it so their parents wouldn't have to buy shoes for the better part of half a year. Saving the cost of a pair of shoes was important when your family was barely making a living on a small East Texas farm.

The first days, until our feet toughened up, were brutal. Every pebble felt like a big nail and every twig like a butcher's knife. Even the soft new grass seemed rougher than a cow's tongue. Our bare feet were nearly always a little cold, enough to make walking on the nails and knives even worse. This all set the stage for the best part of going barefoot in early spring, which was putting our shoes on again—kinda like hitting myself in the head with a hammer because it felt so good when I quit. My soft cotton socks and thick leather shoes provided a feeling of warmth, snugness, and security that made it all worthwhile.

A few weeks without shoes and our feet got really tough. Trails with pebbles and twigs seemed smooth, and we could run lickety-split across areas where earlier we could go only at a snail's pace. Our feet never seemed cold, perhaps because of the warmer days of summer. But now we had to deal with a larger problem—the sand burrs and the bull nettles.

Sand burrs are small, low to the ground, and like grass. They appear to provide the soft green carpet that bare feet really love. But each blade of that grass contains dozens of small pods, covered with stickers sharper than puppy's teeth. Stepping on one is enough to bring even the toughest foot to a quick halt. Stepping into a field of them is like walking on a bed of nails.

Bull nettles are larger and more powerful. They grow in bushes up to two feet high and have pretty white flowers in the spring. In late summer and early fall, the flowers turn to seeds the size of an almond, which can be eaten, although they are not at all tasty.

But don't be fooled. The stems, leaves, and seeds of the bull nettle are covered with what appears to be soft fuzz but in fact are tiny needles that sting and irritate your skin, rather than poke or prick like sand burrs. While a sand burr gets one shot that can be seen and carefully removed, a bull nettle attacks with a blanket of fire that can cause a foot or leg to turn deep red and swell like a balloon about to pop. There is no quick way to stop the pain and irritation.

Those plants mainly grew in sandy places, like the area around Grandma's house. The soil was loose, soft, white sand similar to that found on good beaches: the kind of sand that bare feet love when it oozes up between the toes and covers the tops of the feet with a warm blanket, or acts as a cushion against sticks and stones. But the sand also held burrs and bull nettles.

When visiting Grandma in the summer, we—my brother, sisters, cousins, and I—often left our shoes at home. We went out back of her house and climbed around on the horse-drawn farm machines, played hide-and-seek in the barn, stole watermelons that had been planted for us to steal, or otherwise amused ourselves. Sometimes we walked about a quarter mile down an unpaved, sandy road to Aunt Frankie and Uncle Joe's house to visit our cousins, Joyce and Peggy. Wherever we went, trouble met us.

Braving the sand, the burrs, and the bull nettles without shoes was a real test. The sand was hot enough to fry spit. And the dark green grass and white flowers that seemed to decorate the area made it almost impassable.

The feet we thought were so tough really weren't, so what started as play often became torture. We tried to walk in the clear sand to avoid the burrs and nettles, but after several steps, the hot sand began to fry our feet. This caused us to find green grass to walk on, forgetting about the danger lurking in the burrs and nettles hidden there. We soon realized we had to decide—the white-hot sand or the burrs and nettles. There was no way to win. We could only wish for our shoes.

Kit, Cull, and Runt

Times were different without television to fill our evenings and weekends, but this made it easier for people to just enjoy one another. On Friday evenings, Mother and Dad often piled us into the car and drove to visit Grandma and Uncle Roy, the Barrows, Uncle Paul and his family, or other extended family members or friends. We didn't call ahead, as most didn't have phones. We just showed up and were always welcomed.

One of the visits we enjoyed most was with Kit, Cull, and Runt. They were Dad's aunt and uncles—the three youngest of his mother's ten siblings. Kitty (Sicily Ketrina) was born in 1890, Cull (Robert) in 1892, and Runt (Ernest) in 1895, all in the Oak Grove community. They never married, and except for the time Ernest was in World War I, the three of them lived together on the family farm, where they ran a dairy of a dozen or so cows they milked by hand.

I have no idea how the two brothers received those awful names. They must have gotten them as kids and the names stuck. We kids called them Aunt Kitty, Uncle Cull, and Uncle Ernest.

Kitty was sort of plain, though not unattractive: perhaps a little frumpy, a little moonfaced, and a little weathered but with bright eyes and a big smile. She was a great cook, and sometimes in the summer, when we were baling their hay, Dad, Doug, and I feasted on her noontime "dinner" of fried ham, mashed potatoes, mustard greens, and various other fresh vegetables. She could milk a cow faster than anyone I ever saw!

Cull and Runt looked a lot alike. They were both middling-sized men, slender but not skinny, and slightly stoop-shouldered. Both had angular, weather-beaten faces, bald heads, and ears that were a little too big. I don't remember ever seeing them dressed in anything except khaki shirts and pants, and I'd bet a day's pay neither one ever owned a suit. Cull was outgoing and friendly, while Ernest was quieter. Uncle Ernest was one of only two or three people I knew who had been outside the United States. While he was friendly and sincere, it always seemed like there was something that he didn't want people to know about. I always imagined it was something from the war, or a failed romance, or a desire for a different life. Perhaps that's just the way he was.

Our family enjoyed visiting the Porter's home, particularly on cold winter evenings, when they always had a roaring fire of dry oak logs in their fireplace. We sat in a semicircle around it, enjoying the heat and one another. The adults talked and the kids mostly listened. Usually Kit, Cull, and Runt talked at the same time. I'd like to say they sounded like a well-rehearsed chorus, but they actually sounded more like three hogs fighting over two ears of corn. Dad used to say, "When God passed out manners, Kit, Cull, and Runt were off fishing on Piney Creek." But they were interesting, sincere, and loving—just the kind of uncles and aunt you want to enjoy a roaring fire with.

They planted a big patch of watermelons and cantaloupes each spring, and by midsummer there was a feast for humans and hogs. They raised so many of those big, beautiful, juicy, sweet Black Diamond watermelons that they didn't know what to do with them. So, they just stacked them in a huge pile in the shade of a big tree just south of the barn and next to the hog pen. The melons were for visitors and for the hogs that seemed to always be eating. On our summer visits, we usually got a long knife that Ernest had hidden away in the barn and cut a melon open, took out the very center that is sweetest and without seeds, ate it with our hands, threw the leavings over the fence to the hogs, and went back for another one. It's hard to say who enjoyed the melons most, or who had the worst table manners.

The best watermelons were those we stole. We kids never dared steal them from anyone other than Cull and Runt. I suppose deep down we knew we weren't really stealing when they planted them with us in mind. In any case, we would run into their patch, find the biggest melons around, "thump" them to determine if they were ripe, and carry them to the nearest shade tree. We never had a knife, or if we did it was too small to make a dent in such big melons. So we would hold a melon as high as we could and drop it. Problem is, melons grow in soft, sandy soil, and sometimes the things won't bust when they hit the ground. When this happened, we just grabbed another melon and dropped one onto the other. Then we gouged out big hunks with our hands and had a feast.

My favorite memories of Cull and Runt are of times we were having trouble in the hayfield. I can see it now. We baled hay yesterday but didn't have time to haul the bales to the barn. The weather is turning sour. The sky is dark and we can smell rain in the air. Dad is fretting, "We gotta get this hay hauled in before the rain comes. Just a little rain will ruin all these bales. We better get to work and do what we can. Let's go."

After we have loaded a few bales, Doug, looking in the direction of the barn, says, "Who is that comin' down the road? I can't tell for sure but it looks like Uncle Cull."

Sure enough, Cull and Runt are riding to our rescue. Cull is driving his bright red Farmall tractor as fast as it will go, pulling a big trailer behind. Ernest is standing in the middle of the trailer, holding a rope attached to the frame to maintain his balance, putting me in mind of a bull rider trying to keep from being bucked off. We aren't so sure his older brother isn't trying to throw him. As they arrive in a cloud of dust, Cull asks, or says, we aren't sure which, "You guys need a hand?"

Runt mumbles, "Come on you guys. Cut out all the gabbing and let's get to work," as he heads toward the first bale. They work until all the hay is safely in the barn. Then they just disappear in the direction of home. They expected nothing and the most they accepted was a simple thank you. They helped because we needed help.

Champ

"SOLD! For fifteen dollars. To Fred Blackard, there in the back row."

It was winter of 1952, and Dad was at the cattle auction in Mt. Pleasant to keep an eye on the sale of some of his calves. As he sat on a wooden bench in the big room surrounding the small auction ring, buying a horse was the last thing Dad could have imagined. But there it was, a perfect first pony for us kids. The horse turning in circles in the ring was small and thin, even scrawny. His shaggy coat showed traces of gray and made him appear old. He no doubt was already trained to be ridden and gentle enough to be around small kids. That's about all Dad observed in the thirty seconds or so the animal was in the auction ring. But Dad wanted to get us a horse and the price was right. So, he waved his hand above his head and bought us a horse.

The seller found Dad and said, "Mr. Blackard, you've bought a fine young colt there. Only six months old.

Gonna be a big horse when he's grown—mostly Tennessee Walker blood. Both his parents are big, strong horses. He'll be smart and fast. You got a real steal."

Dad answered with disbelief. "You're kidding! I thought it was an old nag that would be safe for my kids. Not a colt that would grow up and possibly be dangerous."

Dad had missed some signs of youth in the short time our new horse was in the auction ring: a belly that was straight rather than sagging, hoofs that were smooth and rounded rather than rough and cracked, and eyes that were bright and alert, darting from side to side from fear of all the noise and activity. Instead of a gentle old nag that would be as safe as a carousel horse, Dad had purchased a young, untrained colt that would grow into a large, spirited, and possibly dangerous animal. What a deal! Dad loaded him into his trailer and brought him home.

We kids were surprised and excited. After arguing over names for the better part of two days, we agreed to call him Champ. Although he belonged to all of us, as the oldest and largest of the four kids, I felt a strong sense of ownership and no doubt acted like Champ was mine. A couple of years later, Dad bought a second horse, and Doug and I convinced our sisters to give the new horse to Doug and Champ to me.

Back to that first day. Dad's mistake put a huge smile on my face, as a spirited young pony that would grow into a real horse sure was better than an ancient, over-the-hill nag. The only problem was that the colt was too young to ride, and waiting on him to get big enough would be like watching grass grow. But we began the slow process of getting acquainted.

A couple of months later, Santa brought a small, used saddle that fit both Champ and me perfectly. Although the colt was still too young to ride, I nagged at Dad until he gave in, allowing as how, "I guess you're small enough that your weight won't hurt him. Hopefully Champ is small enough that he won't hurt you. So you can give it a try and let's see what happens."

Saddling a young colt for the first time is usually not easy. Although Champ had a gentle nature, accepting a cold steel bit in his mouth, a funny-looking leather saddle on his back, and a tight cinch around his belly would be a frightening experience.

Champ was in a small pasture down by the barn that Dad used as a milk shed. He let us approach and pet him with no problem. Dad walked up to him slowly, petting him, saying time and again, "Com'ere Champ. Everything's okay. I'm your friend. This is gonna be fun." Though Champ rolled his eyes and jumped around a little at first, he accepted the saddle and bridle. When they were in place, I led him slowly around the barnyard several times so he could get used to the bridle and saddle.

Finally, it was time for me to climb into the saddle. Would Champ accept me or would he throw me? If he ran, could I stop him? Anything could happen. Although I was shaking in my boots, I approached him gently, rubbed his arched neck, talked to him in low, assuring tones as I had seen Dad do: "C'mon Champ. It's gonna be okay. I'm not gonna hurt you. You're my friend."

Champ didn't answer. I climbed aboard, with Dad's help, as gently as possible. Champ didn't buck. He hardly seemed to notice I was sitting on his back. Dad led us around the barnyard several times, enough for both of us believe this was going to work.

"He seems to be okay. You ready to try it on your own?" Dad asked, as we were walking what seemed like the umpteenth circle.

"I think so," I said, with a hole in my stomach and my heart in my mouth. "I think we'll do okay."

"If he runs, hold on tight and don't fall off. Have fun."

Dad let go, and the two of us were on our own, with neither knowing who was in charge. To my great relief, Champ didn't buck or run. Instead, he headed across the pasture in more or less whatever direction he chose, at a slow trot that was so bumpy it made my guts feel like scrambled eggs. Just as I was becoming confident that training a horse was easy, we approached a little ditch—about six inches deep and a foot wide—that I could easily step over. I prepared for a jump like those I'd seen Roy Rogers do in western movies. Champ didn't jump. He spread his front legs, put his head down almost to the ground, and came to a jolting stop. I shot like a cannon ball out of the saddle, over his head, and landed on the ground in a crumpled heap.

I wasn't hurt, and Dad insisted that I get back on and ride some more, which I did. I'll never know whether Champ stopped so quickly because he was afraid to jump that little ditch or because he wanted to get rid of me.

Champ grew into a horse that was tall, powerful, and spirited; with a broad, flat back; muscular hind legs; and sparkling, alert eyes. He had a sleek strawberry blond coat during spring and summer, although during winter his hair looked shaggy and unkempt. He grew faster than I did, so we made quite a sight: a small kid perched on the back of an oversized horse. For several years, I had to lead him to a tree stump, porch, or other raised platform to get on him. He became an okay cow pony that we used to herd cattle.

But Champ's main purpose was for play. Sometimes we just rode, and sometimes our activities

Cowboys

were more organized. Several neighbor kids also had horses. We met from time to time at the Texan Theatre on the town square for a cowboy movie, and during the following weeks, we reenacted the movie in the fields surrounding our houses.Champ and I became friendly sidekicks and had a lot of fun as we grew up together, but two scary events could easily have ruined all the good times. The first occurred on a short ride one spring afternoon after school. It was a messy day. Dark clouds hung low in the gray sky and the scent of rain perfumed the cool, humid air, but I wanted to ride and the rain wasn't falling yet. So I saddled Champ and took off, riding slowly down the edge of the farm-to-market highway that ran near our house. The storm exploded after we had gone only a half mile or so. Suddenly, the gray sky became dark, and the wind began to blow in gusts. Zigzags of lightning shot through the dark sky, followed quickly by loud, deafening claps of thunder. Huge drops of rain began falling, slow and scattered at first, then faster, closer, and heavier. We would get drenched in a hurry if we didn't get back to the barn.

Now getting wet in a spring rainstorm isn't so bad, but neither is it great fun. The growing storm was just what I needed to justify a run back to the barn. "Come on, Champ. Let's go. Whooo-ah! Whooo-ah! To the barn!" Just like movie cowboys did when chasing an outlaw gang, I leaned forward in the saddle and began kicking Champ with both heels and slapping his shoulders from side to side with the leather reins and yelling some more.

Champ responded, and ran at breakneck speed along the side of the road toward the barn. Then he turned to the right to avoid something on the side of the road. I shifted my weight to maintain my balance. The shift of weight caused the saddle to turn and rotate around Champ's belly. I was going under. I yelled, "Whoa! Whoa!" and pulled on the reins as hard as I could in an effort to get him stopped—or even slowed—while at the same time trying to correct the turning saddle. Nothing worked. My excitement and the lightning and thunder and the strange feel of the saddle quickly slipping to the side all made Champ run even faster. I was on a runaway horse, and I was about to have a runaway horse on me.

It all happened so quickly. I fell, hit the ground with a thud, and did a couple of rolling flip-flops, managing to avoid Champ's flying hoofs or any other major injury. My cheek hit a rock, however, and for several days the left side of my face was swollen really big. Champ stopped about one hundred yards up the highway and waited patiently for me, saddle hanging loosely beneath his belly. I got up and walked slowly to him. After I put the saddle back on top, we made our way to the barn through the driving rain. I don't know what Champ was thinking, or even if horses can think. I was thinking that the next time I would tighten the cinch around the horse's belly.

There was another scary event. Champ was gentle as a lamb, and I could usually walk up in the middle of the pasture and pet him. As I became more comfortable with him and my riding ability, I started riding bareback, without a saddle. The feeling of freedom, the touch of the horse's warm back, and the greater risk of falling all made riding more exciting. Then I began riding Champ without a saddle or a bridle. I would walk to him in the pasture, pet him for a minute, lead him by his long mane to a tree stump, climb on, and ride. I tried to guide him by leaning forward and pushing his head in the direction I wanted to go, but the truth is Champ was in control. He went where he wanted to, when he wanted to, at whatever speed he preferred. This was usually okay by me, as I really didn't care where we went, and the faster we got there, the better. Not having a bridle only increased the thrill.

One day, I was riding Champ at a fast gallop with neither saddle nor bridle, in that never-never land between fun and fear. My heart was racing, my breath was short and fast, my stomach felt queasy, I was sweating like a stuck pig. It was like hanging on to a big, fast roller coaster or skiing a little too fast down a tough slope. Then it was no fun and all fear. Champ was sprinting directly toward a big blackjack tree that had large, low, droopy limbs extending several feet in every direction. The limbs were dead—hard, stiff, and prickly—and barely high enough to clear Champ's back, and not nearly high enough to clear me. Champ was in control, and would go where he wanted to go. I yelled, "Whoa! Whoa!" and slapped the side of his neck, but he didn't stop or turn.

I'll never know whether or not that horse was intentionally trying to get rid of me, but that's what happened. He ran under the tree limbs and scraped me off. I toppled backward over his rump into a crumpled heap on the ground, my arms scratched from the tree limbs, my body bashed from the fall, and my pride injured once again. Champ ran on. Fortunately, no major damage was done, but after that, I checked for trees with low- hanging limbs before getting on a horse without a saddle and bridle.

Picking Peaches & Fighting Wasps

Early summer usually brought Doug and me a working vacation—if you call spending your days in hot sand, from daylight to dark, fiddling with stingy fuzz-covered peaches a vacation.

Uncle Lavern and Aunt Kitty, Dad's sister, had a peach orchard near East Mountain, a small community about forty miles southeast of Mt. Pleasant. The orchard had acres and acres of peach trees, and a big tin-roofed packing shed where they were brought after picking to be put in baskets and sold to the public. Unfavorable weather often prevented them having much of a crop, but every year or so they would have more peaches than you could imagine, with a slew of them getting ripe, then overripe, then rotten if they weren't picked and sold on time. Those years we had our summer "vacation." They needed every hand they could get for a few weeks—even hands that would rather play than work. Doug and I, along with our cousin Don, were usually asked to help. We lived with Aunt Kitty, Uncle Laverne, and cousins Bill and Sue, had Wheaties and fresh peaches every morning for breakfast, and worked all day doing stuff in the orchard.

Kids had several jobs in the peach business. Sometimes we drove tractors, pulling low, two-wheel trailers, delivering crates of peaches from the pickers in the orchard to the packing shed. Sometimes we picked peaches, sold them to customers, or did odd jobs. Sometimes we just goofed off. Goofing off involved a variety of activities, both during and after the work day: having tractor races through the orchard, throwing rotten peaches at one another, gorging ourselves on fresh peaches, skinny dipping in a stock pond, trying to make peach brandy from overripe peaches. Or waging wasp wars.

Wasps are considered among the most intelligent insects on earth. They build their nests by chewing old wood and plants into a paper-like mass, which they use to build rows of cells much like those in a bee honeycomb. They attach their nests under porch roofs or rafters or in trees or bushes. Large nests can be home to hundreds of wasps. They can give a person painful stings, but they don't sting unless they are bothered or frightened. But when they are bothered, wasps become monsters.

"Guess what I saw today? A big, juicy wasp nest hanging in one of the trees over near the back of the orchard. It's time for war," Don announced, just as we were finishing our supper after a day of work.

"Let's go. But first we've gotta find some paddles," I answered, as I scooped in the last bite of Aunt Kitty's peach cobbler.

"There should be some boards out in the packing shed. We've got some old crates that will be just right," drawled Bill as he jumped up from the supper table and headed out the door. Bill was a couple of years younger than me, about Doug's age, with big, expressive eyes, a freckled nose, and noticeable ears.

We all followed and looked around the packing shed until we found a crate with sides of quarter-inch-thick boards, about four inches wide and two feet long. We got four of the boards and used Doug's pocketknife to carve a handle on one end of each of them. Our weapons were ready.

"Hope I can find it," said Don as we started walking toward the orchard. "I saw it today when I picked up a load of peaches. It was just right for a war. About six feet off the ground, the size of a huge pancake, and loaded with big, fat wasps."

Doug responded, "Let's go, before it gets dark. We've gotta be able to see those suckers so we don't get stung."

Don led the way, through the maze of look-alike peach trees directly to the one with the army of wasps minding their own business. "There it is, just like I remembered. Let's go." The battle started. Don, Bill, Doug, and I on one side. Hundreds of wasps on the other.

A wasp war is pretty simple. You frighten or annoy the critters by throwing something at their nest—not to knock it down, but to stir up the wasps. A big fist full of dirt works best. You do it again and again until the wasps get all mad and start to chase you with the definite intent of stinging. You run as fast as you can— hopefully faster than the wasps fly. Usually several chase you at once. You run until you think—hope— that all but one have stopped chasing you. Then you stop, turn, and fight. You try to swat the wasp out of the air. Then you go back for another attack.

Things often go wrong. Sometimes a wasp flies faster than you run. Sometimes several chase you farther than you expect them to. Sometimes you can't see them quickly enough after you turn to fight. Sometimes you swing and miss. Sometimes you get stung.

And sometimes, the older boys try to take advantage of the younger ones. We had battled the wasps for some time, no one had been stung, and we had killed several wasps. But the fight was becoming more dangerous. The wasps were getting more and more agitated, and some were now flying everywhere look-ing for us and attacking from unpredictable directions. I said, "Doug, I've got a good idea. I'll stand right here. You throw dirt on the nest and make them chase you. Run right by me. I'll knock them out of the air before they get you." I can't remember if it was Don or me who made the suggestion, but it sounded good to me—as long as Doug was the bait.

"No way. You get them to chase you and I'll knock them out of the air." Doug was younger, but he was smart. After arguing back and forth, we agreed to take turns as the bait. Three of us got in line at a safe distance from the nest. Then the fourth harassed the wasps until they chased him and he ran past the line of the other three. Someone nearly always swatted a wasp. Then someone else became the bait.

"Run! Run! He's right behind you."

"Son-of-a-gun's gonna get you."

"OH! *$?# They're coming after me. Get 'em! Quick! Before they get me!"

"Owweee!! He got me!"

"Don't run! Stop and fight like a man."

"Man, that hurts."

We continued our war until dusk, when seeing the flying wasps was difficult and they had what we deemed an unfair advantage. Then we walked slowly back to the house, hot, sweaty, tired, but happy.

Frog Gigging

Ronnie Russell and Dicky Caldwell were friends from Bridges Chapel, another wide place in the road with a store and a school about three or four miles from Greenhill. We became friends while competing against one another in school sports and enjoyed doing things together, like gigging frogs on warm summer nights. Ronnie was about my height but a little heavier, almost chubby, with a flattop haircut, deep-set eyes, a big nose, and a wisecrack for every occasion. Dicky was a string-bean—thin, rangy, spindly-legged, and a good five inches taller than either Ronnie or me. He always played center in basketball. Sometimes they put me in mind of Mutt and Jeff. On this night, both were dressed in their best frog-gigging attire—their oldest blue jeans, a white T-shirt, a pair of well-worn boots, and an old gimme cap.

Ronnie half-yelled as he walked up to our front door, "Hey, Blackard. You ready to go? We've got the gig, but we need another flashlight. You got one?"

I answered, "Where've you been? I'm ready. I have a small light with a weak battery, but it'll be better than nothing. Let's go," as I slammed the screen door at the back of our house.

Dicky, a year older and wiser, said, "Who's got the sack? I have a feeling we'll need a big one for all the frogs we're gonna catch."

"Not me," said Ronnie.

"I don't either. But I'll get one," I said as I ran toward the barn about 150 yards away to get an empty one from the feed bin.

When I returned, we all piled into Dad's old Dodge pickup—the gray one with the bent fender, the hand-me-down that Dad purchased from Granddad Jones for a couple hundred dollars—and threw our gear into the rear. We were all too young to get our driver's license, but that didn't stop us from driving in hayfields, corn fields, pastures, on isolated country roads, and wherever we needed to find frogs. Tonight, we planned to visit several ponds, and they were too far apart to walk.

I drove the truck down the path toward the lake in the middle of our farm. Dad had hired a man to use a bulldozer to build a dam between two small hills. High grass, weeds, and occasional willow trees grew around most of the lake's edge. The shallow end was filled with big lily pads with pretty white flowers. This lake was our favorite watering hole. We fished in it. We watered the horses in it when we were baling hay. Cows drank from it and peed in it. The four of us kids learned to swim in it, and Doug and I often went skinny-dipping in it. On one occasion, Uncle Joe brought cousins Joyce and Peggy for a swim and surprised us while we were skinny-dipping. We stayed under water—the muddiest we could find—while we convinced them to stay in their car until we got dressed. Tonight, we hoped to find frogs in it.

I drove to the edge of the lake and we got out, quietly gathered our gear, and stalked single file toward the dam. We all had flashlights, I had the sack, and Ronnie had the gig. The gig was like a metal hand on the end of a ten-foot-long pole. The hand had sharp, curved fingers that were open while we were looking for frogs. When we found a frog, the kid handling the gig poked it with the contraption and a trigger-and-spring device popped the fingers closed, hopefully tightly, around the surprised frog. "Be quiet," said Dicky. "I hear them croaking. Don't scare them away."

We pointed the beam of our flashlights on the line where water met land—which is where frogs usually sit—as we crept slowly through the high grass and weeds. Dicky muttered, half under his breath, "Someone strike a match to see if Kirk's flashlight is working."

Ronnie, walking at the rear, gig ready, said, "Look

for the whites of their eyes. They sparkle like diamonds. Can't miss 'em."

I hoped we also couldn't miss the water moccasins. Just a few days earlier, I had seen two swimming across the water. I wondered where they were tonight.

"Stop. Be quiet. I see one. Right there—in front, just under the weeds by the edge of the water. Looks like a big one. Ronnie, you ready?" said Dicky, as he caught the reflection of light from those sparkling eyes.

Our hearts skipped a beat. Ronnie stepped quickly to the front—trying to do so silently. "I'm comin'. I'll get 'em." He held the gig about a foot from the frog, with the long pole swaying slightly up and down, in perfect rhythm with his heavy breathing.

"Ker—plash." "What the heck happened?" The frog leaped just as Ronnie pounced.

Now I was using the gig as we crept through the high grass, without seeing either a snake or a frog. Then I saw a big green one, sitting in the grass just above the water line. "Hold it. I see one. Put your lights on it and I'll get him." While Ronnie and Dicky trained their lights, I sneaked around so I could attack from behind, hopefully without the frog spotting me. I lowered the gig, which swayed up and down with my heavy breathing like it had with Ronnie's. I silently counted, "One, two, three," and jabbed the gig at the frog. The gig skipped over the frog's back and the fingers closed around nothing but water.

We finished the lake and visited several smaller ponds. When the evening was over, we had captured fifteen or twenty frogs—some big ones and some almost too little to cook. Our sack jumped around like a kid with the itch. Finding the frogs, sneaking up on them, gigging them, and lifting them out of the water in the gig, then releasing them into the sack, had been a real thrill. We congratulated each other with high fives.

The whole idea of this expedition was to catch enough frogs to have a "frog leg fry," and we succeeded. Ronnie took them home and put them in his mother's freezer.

A couple of weeks later, on Friday night, Ronnie's mother fried the legs, and we ate them along with a big batch of new potatoes from her garden and corn on the cob.

4th of July

I think the Fourth of July is as much about summer, family, food, and unlimited soda pop as it is about country and patriotism. I guess that's because we always spent Independence Day at the Jones family picnic.

One year—when I was about thirteen—we left the house around nine in the morning. All six of us piled into the faded gray two-door Chevy and drove the fifteen miles to Granddad and Mama Ruth's house. The temperature was already above eighty-five degrees and the air scarcely moved. We kids crammed into the back seat of the car and immediately began complaining—about the heat, how close someone was sitting, someone's foul breath, whatever. The complaining would have been worse if we hadn't been so excited about the day ahead.

Dad drove cross-country on narrow oil roads and then headed north on the Talco highway. About a mile before town, just past the broken-down sawmill on the left, he turned right across a small bridge to our grandparents' house, the site of the picnic again this year.

Several cars and pickups were already parked in the shade of some big oak trees near one end of the lake that formed a "C" around the large, red-brick ranch house. The grass on the lawn and around the lake was freshly cut. A long line of picnic tables had been placed under the trees nearest the lake. Two of my uncles, Johnny Paul and Billy Jean, were walking from the house toward the tables, straining under the weight of a large washtub.

"I'm thirsty. I need something to drink," said Donna, before Dad even stopped the car.

The other three of us said, "Me too." Dad listened quietly for a second, then said, with a smile on his face, "What do you suppose is in that tub Billy Jean and Johnny Paul are carrying?"

"Soda pop," we all answered at the same time.

Dad said, "Go for it," as we all jumped out of the car.

We raced to the tub. The time was around 9:30 a.m., and we all had our first soda pop. I started with a RC Cola.

A steady stream of mostly packed automobiles continued to arrive. I don't know how many people came, but there were more than a bunch. Just my grandparents' kids were more than a bunch—eleven, plus several with spouses and children of their own.

Then there was the rest of the Jones clan—Granddad's extended family. And the Mayfield clan—the family of Mother's mother, who had died in childbirth when Mother and three of her siblings were small. And the Cato clan, Mama Ruth's extended family. And a few more distant relatives, plus several invited friends. They came mostly from Talco, but also from places like Deport, Hagansport, Sugar Hill, Paris, and Mt. Pleasant. There were even a few from up around Dallas.

I enjoyed my second soda pop, a Grapette.

Around 10:30 a.m. another uncle, Jerry Lynn, built a wood fire around a big black cast-iron wash pot— the kind people used to boil their clothes in—placed a short distance from the line of picnic tables, which were beginning to be covered with food. When the fire was going strong, he dumped several gallons of home cooked lard into the pot. The lard melted quickly into a cooking oil of sorts. Jerry threw a match into the oil, but it didn't ignite. A few minutes later he threw another match in. It flashed immediately, telling him the oil was hot enough to fry big hunks of fish without making them soggy.

The day before, Jerry had gone to an old man's house over on Sulfur River and purchased several big catfish the man had caught on his trotline. The fish had been cleaned, cut into small pieces, and covered with cornmeal. Jerry dumped a batch into the boiling lard, spattering hot oil everywhere. When the pieces were golden brown, he used a big strainer to remove them. And another batch. And on and on.

I had a Dr. Pepper.

More than people arrived in all those cars and trucks. Yes, they all brought cousins to play with. Great aunts to tell us how much we'd grown and how big we were getting. Great uncles to ask what we were doing during the summer. But they also brought food: potato salad, green salad, pasta salad, coleslaw, tomatoes— both sliced and fried green—fresh green beans with new potatoes, fried okra, boiled okra and tomatoes, black-eyed and purple-hull peas, fresh corn, deviled eggs, baked pork and beans, fried chicken, and all sorts of other goodies. Gallons of sweet tea. And desserts: cakes, pies, cookies, candies, cobblers. You name it, it was there. The tables could barely handle the weight.

Aunts and uncles and cousins and all sorts of family members continued to roll in. We kids always looked forward to spending time with Cato and Virgil, our uncles, but more or less my age. And cousins Janell, Lana, Charles, Phil, and Bruce, as well as cousins of cousins.

I drank another coke.

"Okay guys. The game is on. Harold and I are ready to play." Lon, still another uncle, had dug two holes— about two inches in diameter and thirty feet apart—on a flat area of ground in a shaded area and was starting the annual washer tournament. Except that in this tournament, players pitched silver dollars instead of washers. Since Granddad was president of the Talco bank, and most of his adult sons were in banking, silver dollars were somehow easier to get than washers. F.A. and Farris accepted Lon's challenge, and the contest was on. The game was scored with one point for closest to the hole, three for leaners, and five points for a hole, as I recall. The tournament lasted most of the day, with winners continuing to play until another team beat them. I didn't play too much.

I did drink a Pepsi Cola.

Just before noon, Granddad brought out the barbecued goat he had purchased from a rancher up near Bogota. A whole goat, cooked to perfection—they said. Someone said they thought it tasted like chicken. I preferred the fish.

I had an Orange Crush.

Dinner was ready at noon, and Granddad asked the same blessing he asked before every meal.

The plates were hardly big enough. Thank goodness for seconds—and thirds. I heaped my plate with fried fish, potato salad, and several other great dishes, and topped it off with another Pepsi. And went back for seconds. And sampled several desserts.

Things weren't so hectic after dinner. The day had gotten hotter, and most everyone was stuffed as a

Thanksgiving turkey. It was nap time, but most people just sat and talked. A few continued the washer tournament, and a couple played catch with Virgil's hardball. Two or three kids tried their hands at fishing in the lake—with no result. Granddad sat silently, smoking his big cigar.

Around two o'clock—still full as a tick on a big dog—I walked slowly by Dad and Uncle Farris, who were sitting in folding chairs under the best shade available, talking cows, kids, or both. Uncle Farris was a favorite uncle—a little on the stocky side, round-faced, bright-eyed, balding, always with a good story and ready to laugh and tease. When Dad saw me, he said, "Kirk, come over here a minute. We need a favor."

As I walked over, Uncle Farris said, with a sparkle in his eyes that I missed, "How about picking up those empty pop bottles there by the tree and taking them to the tub where they should have been put. We need to keep this place as clean as we can."

"Okay." I grabbed the bottles and headed at a snail's pace to the tub. Now that tub just happened to be near the one with the full bottles of pop. I got a Coke this time. I took a few sips, walked around behind a car, and poured the remainder of the bottle on the ground.

Dad and Uncle Farris had bet whether I could get that close to the pop tub without having another one.

Of course I couldn't. They set me up. One of them lost, but he should have known.

About four o'clock, just when Dad was getting a little restless and anxious to go home and check the cows, Virgil approached me with an idea: "Hey Kirk. Wanta go see some baseball tonight? The team is playing here. It should be a good game." The team was Talco's semiprofessional team—a gang of men, mostly oilfield workers, who played similar teams in surrounding towns. During the game, the fans passed a hat and took up a collection that was divided among the players, with some extra for anyone who hit a home run. Several of my uncles played from time to time. Johnny Paul graduated from Talco to a AAA club in the Texas League, just one step short of the big leagues.

I responded, "Great. Let's go. But I need to talk to Dad first," as I headed in his direction as fast as I could move with my bloated stomach.

Some serious talk was required to get Dad to stay for the game, because he was ready to go home. I think my final argument was something like, "Dad, we love baseball and never get to see a real game. This is our only chance. You just can't make us miss this chance. We can work tomorrow." Or something like that.

In any event, Dad, Doug, and I went with others to the game while Mother and the girls stayed at the remains of the picnic to continue their visiting and socializing.

About the middle of the first inning, Virgil said, "Hey. Let's pick up some empty bottles. If we take ten empty bottles back to the concession stand, we can get a free soda pop."

I answered, "Let's go," as I picked up one and found another. We spent most of the evening collecting soft drink bottles, and I think I earned three soda pops. I didn't see any of the game, but I heard Talco won. Dad was angry. But what is the 4th of July if it isn't drinking all the soda pop you can hold?

Camping and Fishing

Doug and I sometimes fished at little ponds around the house. Our outing one late spring day was fairly typical. First, we hunted for bait. The weather had been wet and warm, so we expected earthworms to be available. We went to the barnyard behind our house and turned over everything we could find that was lying loose on the ground—a stray board, a feed trough, an old tire. We grabbed a few night crawlers and fat white grub worms before they slithered away, and put them in our Folgers coffee can with a little dirt for protection. Doug also caught a couple of crickets, but after about fifteen minutes of searching, he inspected the contents of the can and said, "This is not nearly enough. There's gonna be lots of fish and we'll need more worms."

I said, "You're probably right. Looks like we'll have to so some digging," as I headed to the tool shed to get Dad's shovel. We dug several holes in the shady areas around the edge of the barn, where dirt and cow manure combined to make a perfect home for worms. But we only found a dozen or so little ones.

Doug said, "These'll be gone before we get started. Let's catch some grasshoppers on our way to the pond."

We grabbed our gear—a couple of crooked poles about six feet long that we had cut from a stand of young persimmon trees, with cotton fishing lines with red and white bobbers, lead sinkers, and small hooks. After a ten-minute walk across the pasture, we arrived at our favorite fishing hole, a small pond near the edge of the woods behind our house. And I mean really small. With all the rain, it was full but still no bigger than a two-car garage, around three feet deep. High weeds growing in the shallow water near both ends made it look even smaller. The water was slightly green. By the end of summer, the pond would shrink and almost disappear. But somehow that mudhole always had little fish in it.

We sat on the roots of the huge oak tree that shaded the entire pond and began fishing. Pushing those squiggly, slimy worms on those little bitty hooks was hard to do, but we succeeded and actually caught a half a dozen: each about four inches long, barely large enough to grab a hook or sink a bobber. We took them home, and Mother fried them whole in cornmeal for part of our supper.

Fishing on Sunday, like working, was against Dad's rules. He used to tell us, "If there's an 'ox in the ditch' it's okay to work until you get it out. But planning to work on Sunday or going fishing is not right. The Lord's Day is for rest." I never quite understood Dad's feelings about fishing on Sunday until I read a short story that his brother, Paul, wrote about a question he had asked their mother: "I remember asking her if she ever knew of anyone who went to the Booger Man (We wouldn't say 'went to Hell.') She said, 'Yes, one time a man fished on Sunday.' To this day I do my fishing during the week." Dad must have heard the same story and, like his brother Paul, wanted to avoid the Booger Man. He rarely fished on Sunday, and we didn't either.

On occasion, however, we did camp and fish over a weekend. Sometimes Uncle Paul and Don, Dad, Doug, and I would be joined by other uncles and cousins, along with Cull and Runt, Dad's old bachelor uncles. These outings usually began on Saturday morning, and we were home by early Sunday afternoon.

Several big lakes have been built in recent years in East Texas, and they are filled with bass, bream, and channel catfish. But in the 1940s and 1950s we had only what nature provided. When we wanted more than a small stock pond, we fished in White Oak Creek, Piney Creek, or Brook's Lake. All three were located in a vast forest area about fifteen miles from home. To get to either of the fishing spots, we took a highway, then an oil road, then a dirt road, then went through a gap in a barbed wire fence and struck out through the woods, usually following a small trail for about thirty minutes. The route was usually marked by large mudholes. I always wondered if we were going to get the car stuck in one of the mudholes and spend forever in that scary place.

White Oak and Piney creeks were similar—little more than long, curving ditches, with oak, willow, bois d'arc, hickory, sweetgum, pignut, sycamore, cotton-wood, and other trees on each bank. Their branches often met over the water and formed a dark tunnel beneath, like one at Disney world. The creeks were always muddy. They were several feet deep and rapidly moving following the spring rains, but shallow and still in late summer and fall. Brook's Lake was hardly a lake at all—only a few feet deep, muddy, little more than a swamp. It was my favorite. Barely larger than a football field, it was the biggest pool of water I had ever seen. We used a small, wooden paddleboat that Dad had paid a local carpenter to build to get around on it.

All three fishing holes were home to catfish. They also held bream, buffalo (fish and not big, brown, hairy creatures), alligator gar (fish with long snouts like an alligator), and more snapping turtles than you could shake a stick at.

One Saturday morning around eight, Uncle Paul and Don met Dad, Doug, and me at our house for a weekend at Brook's Lake. We hitched the family car to our small trailer, built from a pickup bed, and roped our boat firmly inside. Then we loaded the car, trailer, and boat with fishing tackle, an old canvas army surplus tent that we could all sleep in, a couple of cotton sleeping bags, pillows, blankets, pots, pans, skillets, utensils, and other stuff we had sneaked out of the house. And food. We packed pork'n'beans, baloney, Vienna sausage, tomatoes, onions, rat cheese, and white bread for lunch, with extra for supper if it was needed, and eggs and sausage for breakfast. Uncle Paul brought potatoes, and Dad brought cornmeal and lard for frying squirrels and fish if we were lucky. Both families brought sacks of homemade cookies. And a can of coffee, several gallons of sweet tea, and scads of soda pop on a block of ice. The sodas were just about the best part of a fishing trip for us kids, as we drank them when we wanted, all we wanted, until they were gone.

We drove our cars to the lake, staying particularly close together during the last part through the thick woods. There were no campsites—we were in a jungle, not a park—so we found an open area near the lake. It was reasonably flat, on high ground in case of rain, with two oak trees we could string a rope between to hang our tent on.

Once we had selected our campsite, Uncle Paul took charge. "Don, you and Doug help me set up the tent while Fred and Kirk put the boat in the water. Then we'll unload our stuff and make this place a home." We all did what he said.

Dad and Uncle Paul put bullets in their shotguns and struck out in search of fish bait and fresh meat for supper. With luck, they would shoot a rabbit for bait and squirrels for our supper. As they were leaving, Dad yelled, "While we're gone, you guys gather a big load of firewood. And have the grease hot when we get back."

They shot only four squirrels, so we had squirrel stew: a mixture of everything available—the squirrels, potatoes, onions, tomatoes, canned corn—all boiled in a big cast-iron pot until the squirrels, fortunately, were unrecognizable. If Dad and Uncle Paul had been more successful, we would have feasted on squirrel and potatoes, both fried in pork lard in a big black cast-iron skillet over the open fire.

After supper, we set out the trotline. As far as I can tell, using a trotline is fishing for those who don't know how or are too lazy to really fish, but that's what we did. Dad, Don, and I got in the boat and strung several hundred feet of line, with fish hooks hanging every two or three feet, between trees on the side of the lake and stumps or snags out toward the middle. While we were doing this, Uncle Paul skinned the rabbit he had shot that afternoon and cut it into small chunks for bait. Then we put hunks of the rabbit on the hooks. During the night, we took turns "running the line" every couple of hours. An adult and kid got in the boat and checked the entire line—we said to take off the fish before they escaped or were eaten by turtles, but really to bait the hooks after the turtles had feasted on rabbit. I wondered why we didn't call our trip "turtle feeding" rather than "fishing." I didn't get much sleep that night. I went with Uncle Paul to run the trotline around 1:00 a.m. My bed was on the ground, with no padding to soften the rocks and sticks we hadn't removed from our sleeping area. I was bitten by mosquitoes. I got hot in the stuffy tent. One of the adults, maybe both of them, snored like a drunk bullfrog. But mostly it was the coffee. I didn't drink coffee at home, but on camping trips, I did. Dad had made cowboy coffee after supper—grounds directly in the water, in a gallon bucket, boiling over the open fire, terrible tasting, very strong. Lots of milk and sugar made it okay, even better after the third cup. After my second cup, Dad said, "Kirk, that coffee's pretty strong. Drink too much and it'll keep you awake. You probably should slow down."

I answered, "I'll be okay," as I filled my cup again.

Dad said, "Whatever you think."

Of course, Dad was right. My brain was drugged

with caffeine. I made many trips out of the tent to pee. I didn't sleep a wink.

By morning, we had caught five fair-sized catfish, two alligator gars, and a half-dozen turtles. We had fried fish for breakfast. One of the fish was big enough to brag about for weeks.

Our most successful fishing trip was also our most unusual. Rather than fishing with a trotline, a crew of ten or twelve uncles, cousins, and friends used a seine. Ours was a large fishing net, six feet high and seventy-five feet long, with cork floats on the top edge and lead weights on the bottom. The usual idea for seining is to have a group of men on each end drag a seine slowly across an area of water, capturing all the fish in its path except those that are small enough to pass through the holes in the net. Now this works just fine in clean, smooth lakes, but not at all in Piney or White Oak Creek. Thick layers of bottom mud, fallen trees extending out from the banks, frequent tree stumps, limbs floating on the surface, and deep holes and channels made normal seining impossible.

Uncles Cull and Runt, our experts in seining, took the lead. Cull, said, "You guys finish that coffee while I go find a place where we'll catch some fish." The first area Uncle Cull selected had a large, dead tree limb lying at the edge of the water, a hollow tree stump under the water about ten feet from shore, and dark, cave-like holes along the shoreline. The water was about four to five feet deep, on top of several inches of thick, gooey, black mud. Trees on opposite banks shaded the entire area. Water bugs skated across the still surface, and turtles dove off floating logs as we approached. Cull said it was great for fish.

We quietly, slowly—so as not to chase the fish away—encircled the target with the seine. Dad, Uncle Paul, and several other men waded out into the shoulder-deep creek and formed the seine in a "C" from a point on the bank, around the target, back to the bank about twenty yards downstream. Then the fun began. Everyone had an assignment. We kids dove into the center, where we yelled, thrashed, splashed, and otherwise made enough noise to scare the fish away from us and into the seine. The men took their positions around the net.

Suddenly Uncle Joe saw the floats on the seine near him jiggle and sink slightly. He yelled, "Here he is. A big one. Must be a monster," as he made a mad dive to catch the fish with his bare hands. He quickly grabbed a twenty-four-inch-long catfish, wrapped it in the seine, and then carefully removed it into a waiting sack. Several of us gave him high fives for our first catch of the day.

Runt had the scariest job, called "grabbing." He waded into the water and poked around in the hollow tree stump and holes in the creek bank, trying to grab a fish with his bare hands. Hopefully it would be a fish, but more likely a snapping turtle. People said that on a previous seining trip, he had put his foot into a hollow tree, where it was severely bitten by a huge snapping turtle. With no first aid available, they filled the wound with salt to prevent infection.

We moved from location to location and caught several fish, always using the same procedure. Our whole bunch was exhausted and ready to quit well before sundown—wet, muddy from top to bottom, bedraggled hair, exhausted. But the men cleaned the fish, fried them, and we had a great banquet of fish, fried potatoes, white bread, onions, and gallons of sweet iced tea, right there on the banks of muddy Piney Creek.

Saturday Night

We usually listened to the radio for entertainment on Saturday nights. Mainly Dad listened, Mom puttered, and we kids listened some and played some. We tuned in to programs like *Fibber McGee and Molly*, *Amos and Andy*, *Arthur Godfrey*, *Gunsmoke*, and the *Lone Ranger*. The characters were as real in our imagination as characters from television are today.

Our favorite program, however, was the *Grand Ole Opry*. We only had one radio, but the house was small enough that we went to bed, left the doors open between rooms, and all listened to the gabbing of Minnie Pearl, Roy Acuff singing the *Wabash Cannonball*, Hank Williams doing *Your Cheatin' Heart*, Bill Monroe picking *Blue Moon of Kentucky* or *I Saw the Light*, Patsy Cline belting out *I Fall to Pieces*, or Ernest Tubb, Earl Scruggs and Lester Flatt, Porter Wagoner (said by some to have been a distant relative of ours), and many others doing their thing until we went to sleep.

Sometimes the family went to a movie on Saturday night. Mt. Pleasant had three places to go. The Martin Theatre showed mostly new movies, the Texan Theatre showed mainly cowboy shows, and the drive-in movie had a mix.

Babysitters were not a consideration, so Mother and Dad worked us kids into their movie schedule, starting at the drive-in. All of us would pack into the 1945 two-door Chevrolet Fleetline and go to the drive-in out on Highway 271, where we could all get in for the "car" rate. We usually found a parking place up close so we could see as well as possible.

We usually arrived just before dusk on a warm Saturday night. Dad would pay the fee for the car and head toward the front row. Sometimes we sat in lawn chairs in the grassy area in front of the concession stand. This allowed us to watch the movie without some of the drawbacks of sitting in a car, but I think we kids mainly ran around and played, which we could have done at home. Maybe this was the idea—a built-in babysitter so Mother and Dad could see a movie.

When we kids were a little older, the family graduated to the theaters in town. Problem was, Mother and Dad liked to go to the "Martin" and see movies that starred people like Elizabeth Taylor, Rita Hayworth, Tab Hunter, or Marlon Brando. But these movies often involved love stories, kissing, and other such stuff that we kids didn't like. We liked the westerns at the "Texan"—starring Hopalong Cassidy, Roy Rogers, The Lone Ranger, Gene Autry, The Cisco Kid, Wild Bill Hitchcock, or other western actors.

Mother and Dad often dropped us off at the "Texan" while they went to the "Martin." Now our movies were usually a lot shorter than theirs, so we often watched our movie two or three times while waiting for the one at the "Martin" to finish. On more than one occasion, Doug, Donna, Dianne, and I were sitting there beginning the third showing, and I felt a tap on the shoulder and heard someone say, "What's up with you kids. You've seen the show three times and you're the only ones in the theatre. We've gotta shut down. You've gotta leave." We would just wait in the car until Mother and Dad were ready to go.

Then came television. It's hard to imagine not having one, but we didn't until I was around thirteen years old. The first one I remember was at Granddad's and Mama Ruth's house. When we went to their home for dinner on Sunday after church, we often watched Sunday afternoon professional sports, as that's mainly what was available on Sunday afternoons.

Then the Browns, our neighbors a few miles away, got a television. They often invited us to visit, and going to their house for television on Friday or Saturday night became routine. We watched *I Love Lucy*,

Dragnet, *The Texaco Star Theatre*, *You Bet Your Life*, or *The Jackie Gleason Show*, among others. We enjoyed spending time with Bill, Beverly, and Sarah, the Brown children who were about our ages. One of the mothers usually had homemade candy, popcorn, or other goodies for everyone.

Dad purchased a television in 1954 or 1955, if my recollection is correct. This allowed us to watch afternoon shows like the *Mickey Mouse Club* and our favorite westerns like *Gunsmoke*, *The Life and Legend of Wyatt Earp*, *Cheyenne*, *Sugarfoot*, *Have Gun—Will Travel*, and *Maverick*.

Polio

Summers were generally the best time of the year, but they had a darker side during the 1950s. In fact, a very dark side. Polio was a childhood disease where kids had sudden high fever, muscle aches, joint pain, and stiff necks. It killed some of its victims and affected others for life, leaving them with wheelchairs, crutches, leg braces, breathing devices, or deformed arms or legs. The year 1952 was the worst on record, with more than 57,000 cases across the country. The season started before Memorial Day, grew during the summer, and continued well into October.

The fear of polio caused panic in most of the country. Public events were canceled. Swimming pools, movie theaters, and other public gathering places were closed. People drove in stifling heat with their un-air-conditioned car windows closed. Newspapers carried lists of "polio pointers" and other warnings for parents. People feared the terrifying possibility of children being placed for years in a dreaded iron lung, a tube-like chamber that assisted patients with damaged breathing muscles. March of Dimes campaigns and the Mothers' March on Polio gathered money to develop a vaccine and fight the disease.

And then Doug got sick. He had a high fever, muscle aches, stiffness. I don't remember exactly which summer it was, but I do remember what happened. Hushed conversations between our parents. Trying to remember when Doug had last been in the public swimming pool in Mt. Pleasant. Aspirin and cool rags to his forehead to reduce the fever. Several trips to the doctor, a highly unusual situation for us. Doug kept away from the other three kids. No doubt, some private prayers.

Doug got well after a few days. We never knew what the problem was, but we knew a prayer had been answered.

Beavers Bend

Most summers, we spent a long weekend in late August on a family camping trip to Beavers Bend State Park near Broken Bow, Oklahoma, about eighty miles from Mt. Pleasant. The trip was usually an extended family affair, often with several of Dad's brothers, sisters, and in-laws and my cousins Don, Paula, Peggy, Joyce, Bill, Sue, Ann, and Kay. Each year was much like the last one.

We convened at Uncle Joe's house on Friday, midmorning, and headed out in a line of Chevrolets, Fords, and one old Studebaker. Just across the Texas/Oklahoma border, the bunch stopped at a roadside park for a picnic lunch: fried chicken that Mother and Aunt Hollis had cooked the night before, homemade pimento cheese sandwiches, baloney sandwiches, cans of Vienna sausages, fresh tomatoes, plenty of sweet iced tea, and a big watermelon for dessert.

We arrived at the park by midafternoon, in time to find a good campsite and get set up before nightfall—that being finding a campsite big enough to handle us all with two or three convenient picnic tables, erecting our tents and laying out our beds, gathering firewood, and beginning to cook supper. The park was in a beautiful setting of towering timbers, land that seemed mountainous if you had never seen mountains, and a lake that seemed crystal clear when you had been swimming in muddy stock ponds. It also had a swimming hole with a diving board, several swing sets, a couple of horseshoe pits, a big meeting house that was rented for gatherings of various sorts, and a small general store where people could buy things they forgot to bring from home.

We kids spent time exploring, playing games, eating, and just hanging out, although swimming seemed to be the most popular activity, as it also was the best way to beat that Oklahoma heat.

One year, swimming taught me a good lesson. We had just arrived at the camp, and we kids were in a mad race to see who could be the first into the swimming hole. We used our cars to provide some privacy for changing into our swimsuits. I ran to the lake, stepped on to the diving board, jumped high, hit the water surface with a grand splash, and immediately crashed into the rocky bottom, only about four feet below the surface. No major harm done, but I did sport a scratched nose for the next several days. Years later, I learned that Charles Krauthammer, a famous political columnist and Pulitzer Prize winner, became permanently paralyzed from the waist down after a similar diving board accident severed his spinal cord

Occasionally, someone tried fishing, but I don't remember catching any. The adults mainly sat in lawn chairs in the shade, watched the kids, gossiped, and cooked.

By midafternoon Sunday, we were packing to return home.

Baling Hay

Our first hay baler was way behind the times. It was horse powered—a big contraption with an open box to throw loose hay into, a chamber where bales were formed, and an oak tongue to hitch to a horse that walked in circles and provided the power, all on two steel-rimmed wheels with spokes.

Dad purchased it used—rusty and in bad need of fixing—from a farmer near Gainesville who was buying a more modern machine. Dad put the whole mess on a small two-wheel trailer, hitched it to the family car, and drove toward Mt. Pleasant, hoping everything would hang together for the one-hundred-mile trip. He planned to take the back roads and stay as far as possible away from traffic and towns.

But Dad got lost and drove the entire machine—without the horse—down Main Street in Dallas, where skyscrapers shaded his path and curious people in business attire wondered what planet he was from.

The process for using the thing was pretty simple.

We positioned it in a convenient place, typically near the center of the hayfield or under a shade tree. A horse-drawn rake gathered loose hay from the surrounding area and drug it to the baler. Men used pitchforks—five-foot long wood handles with three or four nine-inch-long steel forks on the end to pitch hay into the open box on one end of the baler. A horse walked in a circle, pulling the tongue that worked as a lever to push hay through a chamber, where a man tied it with wire into bales. My first job was to ride the horse to keep it from stopping.

After a couple of years, Dad bought a secondhand gasoline-powered baler. It used the same process as the older one, except that a small motor powered it at a much faster pace than a horse.

Baling hay is hot, dirty work, but I have fond memories of it. A very hot July day in the late '40s, when we were still using the horse-drawn contraption, provides an example. The previous day, Dad had used a horse-drawn mowing machine to cut four or five acres of hay. Now it was dry, ready to be baled.

We got up early to do the "fixin"—to fix what was broken and do all the things that had to be done before we could do the actual job. Dad filled a big steel milk can with drinking water and picked up the dinner that Mother had fixed for us, and we drove in the family car over to Grandma and Uncle Roy's house. We were at

Horse-Powered Hay Baler

Uncle Roy's to fix a broken part on the baler and get his horse and mule team harnessed and ready to go. Dad was ready to get to work and bale some hay. Uncle Roy was still in bed.

Roy, Dad's older brother, had never held a job, left home, or even driven a car. He was small, walked with a slight limp, and had a reddish complexion. When Roy interacted with us nieces and nephews, he ended up picking at us, and sometimes we didn't know whether to love him or fear him. I think most of us felt some of both. People said he had a "condition," but I never knew just what it was. Some said he had polio or a form of epilepsy as a child. Whatever it was, he didn't like working, particularly early in the morning. But Dad needed his team and his tools for baling hay.

So, Dad continually borrowed his tools, which Roy

kept under lock and key. This meant Dad couldn't just pick up the tools. Each time, he had to ask his older brother if he could borrow them. Roy always loaned Dad the tools he needed, but never the keys to open the door to the shop to get them. Only Roy opened that lock, and he did so in his own time, nearly always much later than Dad's.

Dad's views on timeliness were clear: "Time is money. If you're wasting time, you're wasting money. Causing someone to wait on you is taking their time and the same as taking their money. If you wouldn't take their money, don't take their time." But Dad waited on Roy.

In any case, Uncle Roy got up, walked slowly across the barnyard, and opened the door of his wood-frame garage, revealing a big wooden box that held the tools that Dad needed. Dad looked through the toolbox, found what he needed, and repaired a couple of things that broke the last time the baler was used.

After Uncle Roy finished breakfast he fed the team, Hot Shot and Old May. When they finished eating their dried corn directly off the cob, he hooked them to his farm wagon and drove the two miles to the hay meadow, where the rake and baler had been taken the previous day. I went along for the ride, as I considered them almost mine.

Hot Shot and Old May were an odd couple. With a shiny brown coat, white diamond on her forehead, and long, flowing mane and tail, Hot Shot was a beautiful mare in the prime of her life. She was tall and handsome. Her hoofs were so big they could squash a dropped hat or a kid's foot with one step, and her small, alert ears, twinkling eyes, and high spirits made Hot Shot look like a Budweiser horse on television.

Old May was a mule, with a donkey for a father and a horse for a mother. She was almost as tall as Hot Shot, but skinny rather than fat, with ribs that stuck out too much. Her ears seemed too big, and they waggled around rather than stood upright. Though people said Old May was twenty-five years old (seventy-five to humans), she looked even older. Her coat was a splotchy gray and she had the white hair of age showing around her dull, hollow eyes and uncontrollable ears.

The two were a strange partnership: Hot Shot, a handsome young horse with a shiny coat, and Old May, ugly as a mud fence. Hot Shot was big as a barn, while Old May was so thin she could cool in the shade of a fence post. Hot Shot was a worker, while Old May seemed to have been born tired and raised lazy.

In the baling operation, Hot Shot and Old May pulled a rake that dragged cut hay to the baler that was located near the center of the field. The rake

Horse-draw hay rake

appeared to be a monster from another planet. Two thin steel wheels about five feet tall were connected by a twelve-foot-long axle. The driver sat on a tiny seat that was on a stand atop the axle.

Hot Shot was hitched on the right side of an eight-foot tongue attached to the axle, and Old May was on the left—always. They were creatures of habit, and would not work on the wrong side. Curved steel forks attached to the axle could be lowered to the ground, where they gathered the cut hay as the rake was pulled from one side of the field to the other. When the forks were full, the load was dragged to the baler and dumped for baling. Operating the rake was a job we kids could do, as we raced at a fast trot from the hay baler to the cut hay for a load, and then dragged the hay slowly back to the baler before the previous one had been baled.

At the end of each day, Hot Shot and Old May had to be returned to Uncle Roy's barn. I would often ride one and lead the other. This allowed me to pretend I was a cowboy riding a handsome horse and leading a pack mule. I always rode Hot Shot. Old May was so skinny that riding her would have been like sitting on a bouncing razor blade.

Baling hay took a crew of six or seven hands, usually a mix of men and boys. Boys were recruited at an early age to do men's work, and most of us could do a day's work for a day's pay, which wasn't all that hard at the going rate of forty cents an hour. One day's crew was fairly typical. Dad, Mr. Derrick, and James Davis used pitchforks to throw hay into the baler. Uncle Roy set blocks (big wooden blocks were placed in the hay chamber to separate one bale from the next) and pushed wires through grooves in the blocks. Uncle Joe tied the wires into a firm knot when Uncle Roy pushed them around the bale.

Don yelled, "First on the rake!" as soon as we arrived, and he was the oldest of us kids, so he started the day operating the hay rake. I took what remained—dragging bales away from the chamber, stacking them in a pile, and returning the blocks to Uncle Roy for him to use again. Later in the day, when Don and I and the horse powering the baler were equally tired, one of us would ride the horse in its never-ending circle and use

Hayfield

a switch to keep him moving. With an early start and working till dusk, we expected to bale about one hundred bales in a day.

About eleven o'clock one hot day, I looked up and saw James Davis leaning on his pitchfork, staring into the distance with a slight grin on his face. As I followed his gaze into the distance, my heart skipped a beat. To say that Don seemed to be raking hay a lot faster than usual was an understatement. In fact, Hot Shot and Old May were running like greased lightening across the field, and Don, with a terrified look on his face, was yanking the reins with one hand and holding on for dear life with the other, yelling, "Whoa! Whoa!" as loud as he could. It was a runaway rake.

"Dad! Dad! Look at Don. They're runnin' away with him!" I shouted as I ran in Don's direction, as though there was something I could do.

Dad ran in the same direction, but before he could get more than twenty or so yards, Hot Shot and Old May reached the barbed wire fence at the edge of the field. They stopped. Don almost didn't. He actually managed to hold on, get control, and slowly walk the team back to the baler. "Wow! What a ride. Most fun I've had in a long time," Don said. "I got a wasp nest in the rake and they started stinging Old May. She really took off."

By the time the excitement was over, it was almost chow time. We found a comfortable place under the big oak tree near the baler and began eating what under other conditions would have been considered a picnic lunch. Each person provided his own—leftover biscuits and sausage from breakfast, baloney, potted meat sandwiches, rat cheese, sardines, canned Vienna sausages, white bread, crackers, a big onion, or tomato were most common. Dad and Uncle Joe had iced tea in a mason jar wrapped in newspaper to keep it cool, and the rest of us drank the lukewarm water from the big milk can, sharing a dipper. We all had moon pies for dessert. After a hard morning baling hay, anything tasted good, and just a break from work was welcome. After lunch, Dad and Uncle Joe took a nap, and we boys explored a big ditch on the south side of the field.

Lunch time was also important for the horse and mule. Uncle Roy took them to the nearby stock pond, where they waded out belly deep and stood forever sucking in warm, muddy water as though it were from a cool, clear stream. When they were finally finished, Roy fed them a bucket of grain moistened with some sort of syrup, and they helped themselves to some of the hay that hadn't been baled.

We went back to work during the heat of the day and worked all afternoon. I began to wonder if those cows that would eat the hay in the winter were really worth it.

Don and I particularly enjoyed our midafternoon break. Uncle Joe brought two big Black Diamond watermelons that morning, and Dad put them in the shaded water hole at the end of the field to keep them as cool as possible. The melons were the center of attention during our break, although, unfortunately, we didn't have any eating utensils, and the situation got rather messy. Uncle Joe tried to cut those big ol' melons with his little bitty pocketknife, but it barely cut through the rind. He ended up by dropping them on a big tree root that was on top of the ground, which busted them open. We took turns carving out hunks with the available pocketknife and some so-called knives we made from tree limbs. Toward the end, we kids just used our hands to gouge out big hunks of heart. However it was handled, the melon was sweet as honeysuckle and a welcome relief, and we couldn't get any messier than we already were.

Quittin' time came shortly before dusk, in time to get Hot Shot and Old May home and fed before dark. Several of us went skinny-dipping for a few minutes in the pond the team had drunk from and peed in before going home. This got rid of the dust and stingy pollen and avoided trashing the house with our dirty bodies. I can't speak for the others, but swimming was better than bathing in a #3 washtub, so the swim was my bath for the day.

The whole business changed when Dad bought an automatic baler in the mid '50s. Dad, Doug, and I could do in an hour or so what an entire crew previously had baled in a day. Each summer, we baled enough to feed all our cows and began baling for neighbors for twenty-five cents a bale or "on the halves," where we cut and baled a person's meadow and took half the hay for our work. We could put up as many as 1,000 bales a day, which meant hauling the stuff was the real work.

Dad provided a fair amount of hay hauling work for cousins and friends. Pay for hauling was usually around five cents per bale. Three kids could haul four or five hundred bales in a day: not much money for a hard day's work, but better than most kids could get working elsewhere.

Vegetable Garden

The first year or two after our return to Titus County, Dad used Hot Shot to cultivate a vegetable garden. A well-trained plow horse walks in the right place and turns from row to row without any fuss at all. It moves slightly to the right on command of "Gee" and to the left on "Haw." The horse does the work, while the master mainly follows along to hold the plow up.

Hot Shot was not well trained. She didn't know "Gee" from "Haw" and seemed to think tender young vegetables were planted for her to eat or walk on with her gallon-sized hoofs. Sometimes plowing with her destroyed most of the vegetables, no doubt raising Dad's blood pressure. So, he replaced her by buying a tractor to do the plowing.

Dad generally raised a pretty good garden. He started early in the year, even before the last frost, by planting onions, potatoes, and English peas. Later he put in turnips, spinach, lettuce, radishes, sweet corn, carrots, purple-hull and black-eyed peas, pinto beans, cucumbers, tomatoes, okra, squash, and various other vegetables. Last, in early summer, he planted cantaloupe and watermelon. Occasionally Dad grew peanuts and sweet potatoes.

My favorite part was going to the garden on a warm summer morning, pulling a ripe tomato off the vine, wiping it on my T-shirt, and eating it on the spot, with that sticky red juice running down my chin. And using the clean T-shirt to wipe the juice off my face.

The part I hated was picking okra. I'd sooner eat a wasp nest. Okra plants were usually two or three feet tall, with big leaves that hid most of the pods that you eat. The entire plant was covered with fuzz—stingy, irritating fuzz that attacked my hands and arms and face, and then somehow got into my eyes. Then I started sweating and wiping the fuzz everywhere and it all got worse. Today I love eating fried okra or good boiled okra. I swear one reason I like okra is the pure pleasure of being able to eat it without having to pick it.

Digging potatoes and onions in early summer was usually a family affair. Dad ran a plow down each row and exposed most of the goodies. The rest of us picked them out of the dirt, put them in buckets or sacks, and Dad carried them to the trailer at the edge of the garden. He then spread the potatoes on the ground under a big cedar tree with low-hanging limbs and hung the onions in bunches from rafters in the barn closest to the house, where they stayed until we ate them.

The garden created more work for Mother, as there was this feeling that nothing should be wasted. You plant it, it grows, you eat it. You lay by in store. Mother often picked peas or beans in the afternoon, shelled them late into the evening until her fingers almost bled—occasionally we helped her—and canned them the next day. Or canned tomatoes or sweet pickles, or dill pickles or corn. All in glass jars that had to be washed and scalded with boiling water. In a hot, un-air-conditioned kitchen with the gas stove going continuously. In addition to caring for a family of six. I remember more about how hard Dad worked because I was usually there to see it and help with it. Mother's work, like that of so many mothers, was harder for me to see, but that doesn't mean it wasn't there.

Growing Corn

Most years we raised a crop of corn to feed the cows the following winter.

Getting started on the crop signaled the start of a new farming year. The "pop, pop, pop" of the little John Deere tractor straining to pull the big plows through the tightly packed dirt. The cool, soft feel of the newly uncovered soil. The smell of the plowed field. It's late winter, and we are plowing the soil to prepare for planting corn.

We didn't begin raising corn until Dad purchased his first tractor, when I was in third grade. He bought a secondhand "Poppin' Johnny"—so called because it made a loud popping noise that sounded like a bunch of kids popping firecrackers.

I thought I was old enough to drive that tractor from the first day. Dad wasn't so sure, but he couldn't keep me off of it. Even if I couldn't drive it, I pretended: sat in the seat, turned the steering wheel, changed the gears, opened the throttle, pushed the brakes, made goofy tractor sounds, imagined I was plowing or mowing hay. After a week or so, Dad began to let me drive, and before long he expected me to do my share of the plowing.

We had a problem when it came to raising corn. School wasn't out for Dad, Doug, and me until late May, and by late May corn needed to be almost knee high. Since the crop had to be put in on Saturdays and afternoons after school, we had to start preparing the soil early in the year, before the weather turned warm and the soil dried from the winter rains. The first year Dad did most of the plowing, but after that he turned much of it over to me, then to both of us boys when Doug was old enough.

Driving a tractor provided a perfect opportunity for thinking. When you drive a tractor, whether plowing or mowing or whatever, you mainly travel slowly in circles of ever decreasing size or up and back clearly defined rows. Much like traveling in an elevator, it doesn't require any real thought or even much attention. But tractor operation does provide a perfect balance of relaxation and alertness, the ability to be alone without being lonely, that helps us think about ourselves and others. I can't remember much of what I thought about, but I believe those days of quietness riding a roaring Popping Johnny helped shape my life.

The corn growing process was fairly simple. The

ground was plowed three times to get the soil smooth. Then we used a planter contraption on the tractor to drop corn seeds in rows and cover them with loose soil. We hoped for a good "stand," plowed the weeds between the rows a couple of times after the corn started growing, and prayed for enough rain during the summer to make a decent crop.

Late winter afternoons after school often saw Doug or me plowing while Dad was caring for the cows. On one occasion, this presented Dad with a problem. I was working in a field not too far from the hay barn where Dad was feeding. He found a new baby calf, which unfortunately was blind, out in another field. The weather turned foul. Black clouds and angry winds brought hard rain, and hail started pounding, sounding like the inside of a popcorn popper when it hit the tractor. I continued to plow, and the calf just lay where it was. Dad worried—in the barn. He later explained, "When the rain and hail started, I couldn't help both of you and I couldn't decide whether you or the calf most needed my help. Since I couldn't decide, I just let each of you take care of yourself." The calf and I made it with no harm, even though neither of us had the sense to come in out of the rain and hail.

One problem with plowing and planting so early in the year was the wet spots that often occurred in the field. One day I was plowing merrily along, daydreaming, doing whatever you do when you drive in circles all day. Then the tractor was sunk to the axle in mud. And was it stuck! After thinking about the situation, I turned off the tractor motor, walked across the field to where Dad was, and said, "Dad, I've stuck it bad. I'm not sure we'll ever get it out."

Dad answered, "That ground's really too wet to plow. We'll get it out. Let's go."

The ground was too muddy to bring in another tractor to pull me out, which wasn't a problem because we didn't have another tractor. So Dad grabbed a couple of shovels, a big, ten-foot-long oak plank, two fence posts, and a big chain, and we went back to the half-buried tractor and started to work. After a couple of hours digging and pulling and digging and pushing, we finally got that tractor to dry land—only to get stuck again about an hour later. And repeat the process.

Hidden stumps were another problem. Much of the land had been forested in the not-too-distant past, and the trees had been cut at ground level, leaving their stumps just below the surface. When a plow hit a stump, the tractor and you and everything stopped. Immediately. Sometimes you could just back up, lift the plow, drive over the stump, and keep on going. But sometimes the collision bent, broke, or sprained some part of the rig, which typically meant you had to crawl under the tractor and fix it.

On one Saturday morning, Dad sent Doug and me to do some planting while he attended a funeral. I was driving, and had been hitting stump after stump all morning, becoming so frustrated I just wanted to go bang my head against a wall. I hit one more stump. It messed up the rig. Doug said, "There you go again," or maybe even something worse.

I said, "Stuff it," or perhaps something worse, as I raised the plow and backed up, got off, and began fixing the stupid thing. Finally, the rig was ready to go and I lowered the plow and started forward, without thinking where I was. I hit the same stump again. &%XX#$. Doug claimed I blamed him for all those stumps and for my hitting the same one twice. He may be right. I'm sure passing the buck and blaming him made me feel better at the time.

The best part of raising corn was sitting back and watching it grow—and eating the young "roastin' ears" when they were soft and relatively sweet.

Then came corn picking time. We always looked forward to it, but once we got started, we couldn't figure out why. We needed to get most of the crop in before school started, so we did most of the picking in August, when the weather was still very hot. The cornstalks were usually about ten feet tall and thick enough to kill any breeze that might otherwise be stirring. The pollen stung the skin—a little like okra fuzz. The long, thin leaves irritated and sometimes cut bare arms. The plowed soil was hard to walk in and continually filled our shoes. Sand burrs and bull nettles often invaded the field during the summer and stood ready to attack. Otherwise, picking corn wasn't so bad. Unless you had Doug's job.

We drove a pickup down one row, and Dad picked three rows on one side, and I picked three on the other. We pulled ears off the cornstalks and threw them into the truck until we could no longer hit the target, then pulled the truck forward and started over. Doug, as the youngest, was always assigned to pick the "down row" and drive the truck. I can see it now. Doug complained, as he threw an ear so hard it went all the way over the truck, "I don't like this. It isn't fair. I have to bend over all the time and pick up corn out of the dirt. It's hot and dirty. I wanna switch jobs."

I answered, "You're too little. I'm picking three rows to your one. It's time for you to move the truck."

"I don't care. Let's change. Bending over all the time to pick the corn after the truck runs over it and mashes it into the dirt is harder."

"No way. You can handle that job but probably not mine. Get with the program."

Doug was probably right. But tradition had the youngest kid pick the "down row," and Doug was the youngest. I'm glad I missed out on that job.

When the truck was full, Dad drove it to one of three old, broken-down houses that he used to store hay or corn. He backed the truck up to a door and used a big shovel to throw the corn into the house. Doug and I mostly rested and played, although we did relieve Dad occasionally. When the truck was empty, we went back to the field for another load. For several years we filled a four-room house.

During winter, we fed the corn to the cows. Dad threw whole ears on the ground for them to eat. You ought to see a cow crunch and grind an ear of corn—shucks, cob, and all—in one bite. Sometimes we took a truck load and several bales of hay to the feed plant in town and had it ground into meal and put into sacks. We mainly fed this to calves for fattening.

Birth

Several months after we moved into the house at Greenhill, Dad bought twenty-five one-year-old look-alike Hereford heifers, all with red bodies and white faces and stockings. They were delivered to the farm in a big truck, and my family was now officially in the cattle business. By late winter of the following year, we were anticipating our first baby calves.

Every day after school, Dad changed into his old work clothes and drove over to feed and check on the cows. I usually loaded up on crackers and peanut butter and tagged along. One cool February afternoon, even before the car started to move, I asked, "When do you think Slick will have her calf? Do you think it'll be today?"

"We'll just have to wait and see," Dad said. "Maybe she had it last night, and today we'll have our first baby calf."

"I sure hope so. I'm tired waiting." I imagined

a little red-and-white calf that I could put my arms around and hold like a big dog.

Dad thought Slick would probably be the first one to give birth. We named her Slick because her straw-berry red hair was shiny and straight.

My excitement grew as we neared the small pasture within a pasture that housed the sick, the pregnant, and any other cow Dad wanted to be sure was present and accounted for at all times.

The ground was too soft and muddy to drive the car from the unpaved but passable county road to the small pasture, so Dad parked and we walked the last quarter mile. "Do you think the calf will be here? What do you think it'll look like? Wonder if it's gonna be a boy or a girl? Where do you think they'll be? What are we gonna name it?"

"We'll just have to see." Dad was trying to act cool, but I think he was almost as excited as I was.

The waiting was becoming too much—a little like waiting for Santa Claus each year. "I don't see her," I said. "Where do you think she is?"

"Don't know. But if she isn't up for feed with the other cows, that must mean she's hiding somewhere, having her calf."

Slick wasn't with the other cows.

"I'll find her," I shouted, running ahead toward the back of the small pasture. "There she is," I called out a few seconds later, when I spotted Slick lying in the bushes across the branch at the back of the pasture. I bolted in her direction, ducking limbs hanging low from blackjack trees, brushing wild blackberry bushes aside, and vaulting the water in the branch. I was about to be the first to see our first baby calf. My heart was pounding violently.

"Oh, no!" The closer I got to Slick, the more things didn't seem right. She was lying on the ground rather than standing, nursing her newborn calf. No movement.

I was speechless. Dad walked up just as the reality was sinking in. With a hint of sadness and anger in his voice, he said, "We got here too late. They're both dead."

"What happened?" I demanded, tears welling in my eyes.

"Slick did her best but couldn't make it. We should've been here sooner to help her," Dad sighed. "I guess she just couldn't do it alone. Sometimes that's the way it is in the cattle business."

We lingered for several minutes, as though watching and waiting would bring them back to life. But of course, it didn't. Gradually, we made our way to the area where the other cows had gathered and spread bales of hay in silence.

I'm not sure why these deaths affected me the way

they did. After all, they were only a cow and an unborn calf. I realize that my first experience with death was really nothing in the scheme of life. But I remember it well.

One raw, misty Sunday afternoon our family had been visiting Grandma Blackard, just a couple of miles down the road from the pasture where the cows were. After a couple of hours, we said goodbye, just in time to feed the cows before dark, on our way home.

Dad drove the car up the rutted dirt road to the ancient hay barn, and Mother waited in the old Chevrolet with Dianne and Donna while Doug and I helped Dad with the feeding. Eager to get their fill of hay, the cows were restless and fighting for position. Doug and I climbed up a rickety ladder into the barn's loft and shoved bales out the open window to the ground. Dad carried them to the closest clean places in the pasture and spread the hay so each cow could get its share.

After the cows had settled down to eat, Dad counted them to see if any were missing. "... 47, 48, 49.... 47, 48, 49.... 47, 48, 49." Dad carefully counted the cows three times just to be sure. Active cows are hard to count, and Dad finally concluded, as he headed quickly to the car, "One cow is missing. Think it's the white-faced heifer with the brown ring around her eye. Probably hiding somewhere giving birth to her calf. We gotta go find her, and fast. It's fixin' to get dark."

With night fast approaching, Dad drove the car around the pasture to look for the missing cow. Driving was quicker than walking the big field, and the headlights helped us see farther in the twilight. With a little luck the car wouldn't bog down in the spongy, rain-soaked ground.

We crisscrossed the open sections of the pasture while avoiding the low, wet spots, looking first in the easy places rather than where the cow would probably be.

At the back of the pasture was a little creek, impassable by car. Beyond that was a small meadow surrounded by large oak and sweetgum trees, sumac bushes, and wild dewberry vines—an ideal place for a mother cow to give birth in privacy. The search would be difficult in the darkness, but this area was the only remaining possibility.

"Y'all wait in the car, while Kirk and I look along the creek and on the other side. We'll be back in a few minutes." Dad instructed the others as the two of us set out. Glancing my way, he added, "Let's stay in sight of each other, but walk far enough apart to cover more ground."

"Okay," I responded in the bravest tone I could muster. He didn't have to tell me to stay in sight. The last thing I wanted to do was to walk alone on a cold, wet night, in a pasture with creeks, ditches, briars, trees, and who knows what else. Staying close was an easy sell.

We searched along the edge of the creek—walking a few yards, stopping, looking in all directions, listening, walking further. Dad was closest to the edge, as I preferred to stay as far from it as possible.

"Hold it. Did you hear that?" Dad's voice had just a touch of excitement. "Come over here, Kirk. I hear something in the creek. It might be what we're looking for."

We walked quickly to the edge of the creek—really a big gully, eight to ten feet wide, about five feet deep, with both sides almost vertical from years of erosion. Water in the bottom was six to eight inches deep. The creek formed a tunnel, with big trees and dense thickets of smaller bushes and vines along both sides. Dad pushed aside some bushes and we looked in the direction of the rustling noises. There, in the bottom of the creek, lay a young cow, struggling to give birth to her baby calf.

We could see signs of a long, difficult struggle on the bank above her. It looked like she had lain down in a sheltered place beneath the trees and, while wiggling around, had rolled into the creek where she lay, exhausted, covered with muck, scared, cold.

"What a mess. We're probably too late. That calf may already be dead. But we have to deliver it in a hurry or it'll die for sure." Dad spoke softly, as much to himself as to me, as he carefully climbed down into the ditch. "Come around here. Let's see what we can do."

We did all we could, but we were too late. The calf had died during its mother's valiant struggle to give it life.

This wasn't my first experience with a dead calf, but it still brought a tear to my eye. Dad brought me back to reality. "We have a bigger problem now. This cow is really beat. She can't walk or even stand up, and there's no way she can climb out of here. The only thing we can do is get the tractor and pull her out. Hope she doesn't drown while we're gone. Water's rising, and she may be too weak to hold her head out of it."

I knew what I had to do. "Dad, I'll stay here with her while you go get the tractor. I can hold her head up and keep her from drowning."

"You're not afraid to stay? It'll take a while for us to get back with the tractor."

"No. I'll be okay," I claimed.

I stayed with that miserable cow while Dad and the rest of the family went after the tractor. It was so dark I couldn't find my nose with both hands. Cold and scared, I sat in that muddy creek bottom with the cow's head propped on my leg. But I also felt important and warm inside. I was doing something that needed to be done—helping Dad, and helping sustain life, if only a cow's life.

After some time—probably much less than it seemed to that cow and me—Dad returned with the tractor, a long rope, and a big, low sled. We managed to wriggle the rope through the soft mud under the cow and tie a sort of sling around her belly. Dad backed the tractor as close to the edge of the creek as he dared, and tied the rope to the hitch. "You stay with her head and try to hold it up while I pull her out," he instructed. "Yell if there are problems and I'll stop."

"We're ready. Let her go."

The tractor inched slowly forward. The rope tightened, and the cow began to slide across the creek bottom and gradually up the side. I struggled to hold her head up, but slipped and fell. They just dragged me along in the process. We were soon on land—not dry, because of the continuing drizzle—but at least out of the muck and slime of the creek bottom.

Dad pulled the sled alongside the cow's back. He grabbed her rear feet, I her front ones, and we rolled her from the ground onto the sled. My father then hauled the exhausted heifer to the hay barn where this whole saga had started. I followed with the rest of the family in the warm car. At the barn, we rolled the cow off the sled onto a soft, fluffy bed of dry hay.

Though her recuperation was slow, we nursed her back to health over the next several days.

Cows are not the only creatures of God that struggle. Relatives, friends, acquaintances, and people we don't even know often fall into a ditch and need help. The great thing is that helping them helps us even more. We can get that same warm feeling down inside that I experienced while helping that cow and my father. Our life is fuller as a result.

One late spring Saturday, Dad had business in town—I think it had to do with teacher stuff at the end of my third-grade year. As he was gathering his materials before leaving, he said, "Kirk, I'll be in town on business most of the day. That cow in the lot by the barn may give birth before I get back. She may need some help. Why don't you keep an eye on her."

"Okay, Dad," I responded with some hesitation, not knowing exactly what keeping an eye on a pregnant cow meant but feeling too much pride to ask. I just hoped nothing happened on my watch.

Four or five times during the morning, I walked the hundred yards or so to the barnyard to check on her. She was small, dull red with a white face, small horns, protruding belly. Each time I visited, she was grazing contentedly in the small barnyard or standing under the shade of a big oak tree, chewing her cud. When I checked just after noon, I didn't see her at first, and then I spotted her in the back part of the lot, as far away as the fence would allow. She was pacing nervously in small circles. I watched the heifer from a distance for a few minutes. She lay down, got up, laydown again. Finally, she stayed down. Was this her time?

A gnawing feeling arose in the pit of my stomach, and suddenly the cool spring day seemed warm, the breeze seemed to stop, and small freckles of sweat appeared above my upper lip. Was she really going to have her calf now, and what should I do? I had helped Dad deliver a couple of calves, but we had arrived when the situation was obvious, and he made the decisions. This was different. If the cow wasn't in charge, I was. And she didn't seem to be in charge.

Time passed so slowly as I observed the action—or inaction—from behind the corner of the barn, trying to see without being seen. I wasn't at all sure what was going on. Then, I was sure. The heifer was lying on the ground, flat on her side, giving birth to her baby. It all happened so quickly.

I returned to my hiding place behind the barn to watch as the cow took over. She stood, a little unsteadily at first, turned around, and began to explore the new object on the ground beside her. She nudged her baby with her nose and licked and cleaned it with her rough tongue, exhibiting the love any mother has for a child. At first, the calf lay motionless on the soft grass, as though this strange new world had it completely befuddled. After a few minutes, however, the skinny little creature with the big eyes and protruding ribs struggled up on its spindly legs and took a few steps toward its mother. It nuzzled around like it was blind. The calf finally found its first dinner and began to nurse with great vigor while the mother continued to lick its back.

I checked on the couple several times during the remainder of the day. The cow mainly rested, but the baby began to explore its new life a few small steps at a time.

When Dad returned that evening, I gave him a detailed rundown, and he was pleased. I will never know whether that cow really needed my help. But I was there to help her if she needed it. If it didn't help her, it surely helped me.

Winter Feeding

Winter of 1951 was colder than usual. Temperatures fell to single digits at night and barely rose into the twenties during the day. Icicles hung like daggers from roofs and tree limbs. Six inches of snow covered the countryside with a sparkling white blanket. Ponds were frozen thick enough to walk on. Smoke puffed from chimneys, briefly leaving its curving signature in the chilled air before disappearing on the wings of the constant north wind. Titus County was a winter wonderland.

But it was a wicked, miserable time for cows. They huddled together in small groups to share their body heat: backs arched, tails between their legs, noses and eyes running, heads down against the wind. Icicles hung from their long winter coats. If you had milked one, it would have given ice cream. The cows made brief, feeble efforts to graze in the winter wasteland, but mostly they just hung out around the barn, waiting patiently for their daily ration of hay and a few protein cubes and for someone to break the ice on the ponds so they could drink. They depended on us for survival, but the snow and ice made it difficult for us to help them.

Dad had split the herd into three groups—the obviously pregnant cows, those that did not appear to be pregnant, and the calves held over from last year. Each was in a different pasture and was fed at a different barn. Normally, Dad drove the family car to each barn—they were about a half mile off the paved road and about the same distance apart—over a rutted dirt road that was little more than two parallel cow paths. The road, which crossed a couple of small creeks and climbed a slick clay hill, was rugged in the best of times. Snow and ice made it impassable in a car. The only way to get to the barns was to walk from one to the next.

After the drive from our house in Greenhill, the car was warm and toasty. Dad parked at Ed Martin's store, a convenient location to begin our walk. As he stopped the car, he said, "Kirk, it's awfully cold outside. Going to all three barns is a long walk. I can handle this myself. Don't you want to stay in the store where it's warm and wait for me to finish?"

"No. I'll be fine," I replied, without knowing how cold it would be.

"Okay. Let's go. Fasten your coat and put on your gloves. We don't want to freeze," Dad said as he opened the car door. We got out of the heated car and started hiking toward the first barn. Dad walked in one of the ruts and I in the other, our steps singing a duet of pops, crunches, and squeaks as they broke the crusty snow.

I soon realized this was going to be a colder job than I signed on for. The day was unusually cold for East Texas, and we were dressed for a more normal winter day—one that was brisk, perhaps drizzly, but with no snow and temperatures in the high 40s rather than the low 20s. I wore blue jeans, T-shirt, long-sleeve cotton shirt, school jacket, loafers, cotton socks, thin cotton work gloves, and a light sock hat on my head. Dad was dressed about the same way. Great for school, but not nearly enough for walking through snow, throwing feed to hungry cows, and breaking ice on ponds.

My shoes offered little protection at all, and within a few minutes, the snow began to trickle down around my feet, melt, and saturate my cotton socks. My feet began to stiffen and ache, warning that they were about to get really cold. Fortunately, other parts of my body were holding their own. Keeping my hands in my pockets provided an added layer of protection, and my sock hat was working pretty well in the crisp, dry air. But, oh, my wet, cold, stiff feet. By the time we reached the first barn, they were throbbing with every step.

The first barn on our route was a big, dilapidated gray structure, built many years before as the center-piece of a working cotton farm. It had two rooms in the middle for storing cotton or corn, lean-to sheds on two sides for housing livestock, and a big loft under a steep pitched roof for storing hay. We used the entire structure to store hay. When we arrived, I climbed up the ladder to the hayloft and began throwing bales out the open door. Well, I didn't really throw the bales out. I scooted them across the board floor and toppled them out, as my hands now seemed frozen and lifting the bales with the baling wire felt like cutting my hand with a knife.

Dad scattered a bag of cow feed on the cleanest ground he could find and spread the hay around so each cow could get a fair share. He counted the cows to be sure none were missing and looked carefully at each to be sure it was okay.

"Good, the feed's out and the cows are all here and alive. Now we need to get them some water. Let's go," Dad said as he grabbed a big, long-handled sledgehammer from the corner of the barn and started toward the frozen stock pond. Now breaking ice on a stock pond presents a problem. If you stand on the ground, you can't reach enough water to do any good. If you stand on the ice while you're breaking it, well—you fall into the water. Wherever you stand, you're gonna splash freezing water on yourself. But somehow Dad did it.

Dad did most of the work, while I hung around,

helped when I could, got colder and colder. My feet were numb and felt as brittle as the sledgehammer Dad used to break the pond ice. By now, my hands—removed from my pockets to help with the feeding—were almost as cold as my feet. I could imagine one slight blow breaking my hands into dozens of brittle pieces. My ears were beginning to suffer through the light sock cap. And we had two more barns to go.

"That's all for here. Ready to go the next barn?" I wasn't sure what Dad meant. Yes, it was time to go. But no, I wasn't ready. I was freezing. I didn't reply. I just started walking, painfully, through the snow and wind toward the next barn.

Perhaps Dad's question was a test, and I guess I passed—barely. After we had covered just a few yards, he said, "Kirk, it's a long, cold walk to the other barns, and there aren't many cows there. I really don't need help feeding them. Why don't you go back to the store and wait by the fire 'til I'm finished. I'll be okay."

I faked it for a few seconds. "Are you sure you don't need me?"

"Yes, there's not many cows, and I can handle them. Both of us don't need to go," replied Dad, as he dug his cold hands deep into his pockets and turned toward the second barn.

My miserable feet, hands, and ears made the decision for me. "Okay. If you really don't need help, I guess there's no reason for me to go along. I'll just walk back to the store. I am getting sorta cold," I said.

I struck out down the frozen, snow-covered trail, retracing our steps from an hour earlier as fast as I could go. My progress was slow, but visions of the pot-bellied stove and roaring wood fire kept me going.

Ed Martin's store, like Rolf's store in Greenhill, was an ancient, rectangular building about thirty feet wide and two or three times as long. The outside walls were weathered pine boards—the original paint had long since disappeared—running from the ground to the eight-foot-high ceiling, and supporting the rust-ing sheet-metal roof. A big sliding door was midway down one side, and a double door, two small windows, and a drive-through porch were in the front. On one side of the porch were two weather-beaten, wooden benches where customers, neighbors, loafers, and oth-ers hung out during the hot summer months. A single hand-powered gasoline pump was on the other side. Customers used a long handle to pump gasoline from an underground tank into a glass container on top of the pump that was marked to indicate gallons and half-gallons. When they could see the correct amount in the glass tank, they stopped pumping and let gravity drain the gas into their car. Customers told Mr. Martin how many gallons to charge them for.

The store held a little of many things and not much

of anything. Just inside the front door was a small, "U-shaped" counter, with a glass cabinet on the closed end. The cabinet held Twinkies, moon pies, peanut patties, and various sorts of candy for five cents, as well as gum, jawbreakers, and other small sweets for a penny. It also held snuff, chewing tobacco, pipe tobacco, and cigarettes, as the problems from smoking weren't yet understood. One side of the counter provided space for customers to put whatever they had decided to buy while they continued their shopping. The other side held a small, hand- operated cash register and the small charge pad where Mr. Martin wrote down all the things people bought on credit, to be paid for at the end of the month.

The soda pop box was to the right of the front door, beneath one of the small windows. It was about two feet wide, five feet long, four feet high, and bright red, with "Coca-Cola" inscribed on the side. Inside was every kind of pop I could imagine—glass bottles of Coke, RC Cola, Dr. Pepper, Grapette, Big Red, Chocolate, Orange Crush, and others I can't remember. They were in water, cooled with a large block of ice that was replenished occasionally when the delivery man showed up. The drinks went for five cents, and for another five cents, you could buy a sack of salted peanuts to put in your coke and really have a feast.

The side walls were lined from floor to ceiling with

narrow, sagging board shelves filled with canned goods of every sort, flour, sugar, salt, rice, and whatever else would last without refrigeration. A little electric ice-box contained small amounts of milk, a few semi-fresh vegetables, a hunk of rat cheese, and a little baloney or other meat. A separate shelf held white bread delivered every third day from town.

A feed section in the rear contained cottonseed meal, corn, crushed oats, and mixed feed for cows, hogs, and horses. Some of the feed was in large, rough, brown burlap sacks. The remainder was in brightly colored designer cloth sacks, covered with flowers, geometric designs, or other figures. Ladies often decided which sack of feed to buy, as this was when they selected the fabric for their next dress or blouse.

In winter, the best part of the store was in the center: a potbellied, wood-burning stove, filled with roaring oak logs on a bed of red-hot coals. A box of extra logs sat behind the stove, ready to keep the fire going. Hot as it was, however, the stove didn't really heat the drafty old building. Like a campfire, it heated a few feet out but had little effect beyond that. So the stove was surrounded by an assortment of stools and high-backed, cane-bottomed chairs, all loose, creaky, and sagging with wear. People, mostly old men, or at least they seemed old at the time, sat close around the fire until their front began to burn, then stood with their back to the fire and continued their gossiping without missing a beat.

"Kirk! Where did you come from? Get in this house before you freeze." Mr. Martin greeted me as I stumbled through the big front door. I always thought he was a little out of place in that old store. He was over six feet tall, trim, square- shouldered, with a good-looking face and hair that seemed blow-dried before the days of blow-dryers. He was a little too handsome, a little too pleasant, a little too smooth. Should have been a movie star or a politician.

I made my way toward the stove like it was a big magnet and I was made of frozen steel. "What happened? I thought you were with your Dad, feeding the cows," he continued, with just a hint of teasing in his voice as he put another log on the fire.

I was so cold I could hardly respond. My feet and hands felt frostbitten, and my face like an ice sculpture. Would talking crack my frozen face? "I was," I muttered. I was too cold to speak and a little embarrassed that I had returned before the feeding job was complete. "I got so cold I had to come back," was the only explanation I could offer.

"You guys let this man to the stove." Mr. Martin cleared the way for me and insisted I take his chair. All the others were being used, as the day was too cold to work and several men from around the community had gathered to talk, mainly about how cold it was at their place. "Here, take my chair and warm those feet and hands."

I gladly accepted his offer. "Thanks," I said as I sat down facing the stove, feet and hands extended as close to the hot metal as I dared. Soon, I was engaged in the normal rotation—face the stove, burn, stand and turn around, burn, and so on. I gradually began to thaw, regain feeling in my hands and feet, and feel like a normal human being. After I was fully cooked on both sides, I even began bragging about how cold it was at our place and how thick the ice on the pond was.

Dad returned after a couple of hours—freezing from his long afternoon of walking between barns and feeding cows. He also roasted himself. When he was done, we said goodbye to the group, got in the car, and headed home. I felt I had been saved by a warm fire and a friend who invited me to share it. We often need the comfort they provide, and we often need to provide it to others. A warm fire and a kind word usually go a long way toward handling our problems.

Cattle Drive

A cattle drive on a Saturday morning in early October was more fun than work. Doug and I awakened early with no help from Mother or Dad, put on our clothes that most resembled what a movie cowboy might wear, quickly ate the big breakfast Mother had waiting on the table, grabbed our dirty, old straw hats, and dashed out the door. We saddled our horses—Champ and Rusty—and headed toward the back of the one-hundred-acre pasture Dad ran cows on near our house in Greenhill.

We picked our way carefully across the pasture, as it was more like a jungle. A portion was heavily wooded, mostly with large oak, blackjack, and hickory trees. The other part was populated by smaller persimmon and sassafras trees, dewberry vines, sumac bushes, and six-foot-tall clumps of rosin weeds. A little grass was interspersed among all the other stuff. We pointed our horses in the general direction we wanted to go and let them find their way through the maze. Sometimes horses know better than people.

"I don't see any cows. Let's head all the way to the back and then work our way to the gate at the front. That way maybe we'll find them all. Dad said to herd them against the fence and toward the gate, and he'll try to push them through," I said as we approached the heavily wooded area.

Doug kicked Rusty in the side and slapped her neck with his reins, "I'll start at the fence by the railroad track and you can take the middle."

Our job for the day was to find the thirty-five cows that were grazing in the jungle, herd them out a twelve-feet-wide gate onto the adjoining farm-to-market highway, and drive them the four miles to the farm at Oak Grove. They had been grazing in this pasture since June, and Dad wanted them back on the main farm before winter feeding started.

You've heard about "herding cats." Well, herding cats is nothing compared to trying to push thirty-five cows through a near jungle, each with a mind of its own, wanting to graze rather than move, hiding behind trees and bushes, generally being as ornery as a scared possum. Sometimes cows are like people. They want things their way and don't want to be told what to do.

"Oooah, ooohah! Get outta there, cow! Wha! Wha! Move'em out!" Doug and I began finding cows and slowly driving them in the direction of the highway. Move one, then go get another. A few steps forward and almost as many backward. Finally, the cows began to hang together and move in a group toward the fence. When they got to the fence, they turned left toward the gate, just as we had planned. Perfectly positioned, Dad shooed them through the gate onto the highway. What a relief when the last cow passed through. Now we could start the real cattle drive.

"Hey guys. You must'a missed one. I only counted thirty-four as they went through the gate. Didn't see that ol' wild-eyed heifer with the crooked horn. The crazy one that keeps getting out. Better take another ride through the pasture and see if you can find her. I'll try to keep the others together here on the side of the road while you check it out. There's good grass here, so it shouldn't be a problem." That isn't what we wanted to hear from Dad. Doug and I were ready to go and now we had to start over because of one outlaw cow. A slick-skinned, wild-eyed two-year- old that broke all the cow rules. If she had been a person, she would have been in reform school.

We crisscrossed the pasture for about ten minutes and found her hiding in a shaded area behind a bunch of persimmon trees. When she saw us, she bolted— her arrogant eyes bulging, head up, tail flying, bashing through the bushes. Fortunately, she ran in the right direction, toward the highway, with Doug and me in hot pursuit. When she saw the fence, she didn't turn, slow down, or jump. That stupid cow ran right through the fence like it wasn't even there, breaking a wire and pushing over a post in the process.

"Well, that's not what we planned, but at least she's on the road. No tellin' where she's goin' now," I said, as I reigned Champ to a stop just short of the fence.

Doug pointed in the direction of the cows on the side of the road and said, "What on earth is going on up there?"

"Beats me. Let's go see." We slapped our horses and tore out in the direction of the gate.

Cows were everywhere—grazing, moving up and down and across the road. Several cars were parked along the edge, and people were milling around, pointing, and talking excitedly. A car horn was blasting as an impatient neighbor tried to move cows off the road so he could make his way to town. The crazy heifer was still running, almost out of sight down the highway. Two cows were lying prone on the side of the road, swollen up like big balloons that were about to pop. Dad was trotting in our direction, wildly waving his hands, yelling something we couldn't understand. What a mess!

When Dad got to us, he said, "Quick, ride to the house and get your mother's biggest butcher knife and bring it back. I'll explain later."

Dad didn't get excited very often. When he did, we

obeyed first and asked questions later. I lit out for the house, wondering what in the world a butcher knife had to do with all that confusion up on the highway. Fortunately, Mother was not at home, so I didn't have to try to explain why I was taking a kitchen knife to a cow calamity.

I handed Dad the knife, one with a wooden handle and eight-inch blade. Without saying a word, he walked calmly to one of the prone, bloated cows and stabbed the knife directly into the lower part of its stiff stomach. "Whoosh." A gush of air came out of the hole created by the knife. The cow's stomach deflated to normal, and she jumped up and returned to the grazing herd. Dad repeated the process with the other cow and she reacted the same way. The neighbors, Doug, and I looked on in amazement.

Dad explained, "See that big grass up there on the side of the hill? Three feet high, little heads on it, beginning to turn yellow? That's Johnson grass. Sometimes, at just the right time of the year, usually in the fall, it contains a poisonous acid. When a cow eats it, she'll swell up and die in a matter of minutes. It causes a gas that'll kill her. The only thing to do is get the gas out. That's what I did. Looks like it worked. But now we need to get these cows moving before some more go down."

Dad drove the car in front and Doug and I took the

rear, slowly driving the cows down the highway, then a narrow country road, to the main farm. The drive was uneventful—well, except when barking dogs scared the cows, speeding cars scattered them in all directions, or the whole herd headed toward a neighbor's unfenced corn patch. But we made it.

We never did find the lunatic heifer who blasted through the fence. A couple of days later, an irate neighbor called and said, in a very irritated tone, "Hey guys, we've got a problem over here. A strange cow is in my pasture and she's been running around like she's lost her marbles and really agitating my dairy cows. They've about quit givin' milk and I'm losing money faster than I can count it. I think she must belong to you. If she does, you need to get her in a hurry." Sure enough, it was ol' crazy. Doug and I got on our horses and chased her—while the dairy cows were in the barnyard for milking—until she petered plum out and acted gentle as a lamb. We got a rope on her, drug her into a trailer, and took her directly to the sale barn. I don't remember how much money Dad got for her, but it was probably more than she was worth. And the whole episode didn't endear us to the neighbor.

Working Catttle

We had roundups—or at least our version of them—several times each year. The first was usually in late spring, after most of the calves had been born. Most years we rounded up the herd during late summer to spray them with some type of fluid to keep the flies off, and each fall we gathered the herd to separate the calves and truck them to the auction in town for sale. Like trail rides, roundups were an occasion for Doug and me to do some work and also have fun.

Our corral was a net-wire fence enclosure about the size of a baseball diamond that would hold the entire herd. Next to the corral was a pen about the size of an ordinary living room, with a six-foot-high board fence around it. This pen, where the main action occurred, was located under some big oak trees that provided welcome shade on hot summer days.

Our first job was to get all the cattle into the corral. "You guys get your horses and ride the pasture. Drive all the cattle this way and I'll help herd them into the corral." Dad's assignment kicked off a spring roundup one warm Saturday morning in my seventh-grade year.

We replied, "Okay. Get ready. We'll have them back in a little while," as we headed in a slow trot to the back of the place, a good ten-minute ride. On the way, Doug saw a jackrabbit—gray, lanky ears upright like two radio antennas, the greyhound of rabbits—running across the open pasture in front of us. "Let's get him," he yelled as he slapped Rusty across the shoulders and leaned forward in the saddle. In no time, both horses were running full out and we actually gained on the rabbit until it ran through a barbed wire fence, which of course stopped us in our tracks.

The cows were spread in several fields on both sides of the creek near the back of the place, some in open pasture and some in wooded areas. Doug took one pasture and I another, and with a lot of running and yelling, we gradually had them moving in the direction of the corral. Most of them had done this many times before, so they knew where to go. When the herd got to the pen, Dad shooed them in and quickly fastened the gate.

Our first job was to separate the calves from the cows, as the cows got a free ride and were set loose back into the pasture. The forty-two calves were not so lucky. We vaccinated all of them for blackleg, a disease that can hit calves with devastating effect, with a dull needle the size of a big pencil lead.

Dad liked to keep a few of his best female calves each year to replenish his herd. They were vaccinated again, for bangs, a disease that often causes cows to lose their unborn calves.

My fondest memories of roundups involve, of all things, food. Late each fall, we sold the year's calf crop, which of course was the reason for raising cattle in the first place. The cattle auction in Mt. Pleasant was held each Tuesday, so our process started on Monday after school. One Monday in early October was a good example. We corralled the herd like we always did. Then Dad said, "Okay, guys. I'd like to sell about twenty head tomorrow. Let's put the twenty largest ones in the little pen up front."

After a lot of running and yelling and bopping occasional cows on the nose with an oak stick, we had the twenty separated and penned. Then Dad said, "Now for the hard part. We need to find their mamas so we can leave them together tonight. We want the calves to get their fill so they'll weigh as much a possible when we take them to the sale barn early tomorrow morning. Let's see if we can figure out which cows belong to which calves." Some we knew, and sometimes we just turned a cow into the pen to see if she acknowledged her calf, which usually happened. After an hour or so of guessing and watching, we had most of the pairs together. "Good," said Dad as he headed toward the nearby hay barn. "Let's get a couple of bales of hay for them to eat tonight."

Tuesday morning came early. We got up before daylight and drove to the corral in the former ice truck Dad had bought the previous year. It was a badly used, three-quarter ton Chevy with an extra-large bed, and we had built cattle frames of rough oak timbers. Dad drove into the pasture and backed up to the loading chute. We separated the calves from their mamas, drove ten of them up the chute into the truck, and took them to town. After a second load of ten, we drove home for Mother's breakfast before going to school. Mother outdid herself. She served thick-cut bacon fried crisp, eggs fried in the bacon grease, white cream gravy with bacon remnants, fluffy golden biscuits, honey for Doug and me, and ribbon cane syrup for Dad. Over the years, I have enjoyed a big breakfast from time to time. I think this enjoyment started with Mother's breakfasts on those crisp October mornings when we were hauling cattle to the auction barn.

After school, we returned to the auction to watch the sale of any calves that hadn't sold earlier in the day and collect Dad's check. The barn was a big complex that included cattle pens, an auction ring, and administrative offices under one big tin roof. The ring was a half circle about the size of a normal living room, surrounded by an amphitheater where buyers, many from feedlots around the state, came to purchase cattle, and sellers sat to watch the action: a gate opens, a cow enters, a cowboy slaps it on the back with a long switch and yells a starting price, the auctioneer barks some gobbledygook, a couple of people raise their hands or nod their heads, the auctioneer yells sold, and the cow is ushered out. All in ten or fifteen seconds.

The auctions often lasted until well into the evening. In an effort to keep the buyers present and active, the auction management often handed out hamburgers—those really good, fat Dairy Queen hamburgers—to anyone who wanted them. I ate my share. They weren't as tasty as Mother's breakfast but nevertheless were a real treat in the days before McDonald's.

Then Dad collected his check. My recollection is that calves sold for twenty to thirty-five cents per pound at the time, and Dad's were often pretty small, so they rarely sold for more than a hundred dollars, and usually for significantly less. This wasn't much by today's standards, but it was enough to keep him in the business, although I sometimes wonder if that was more because of his poor record-keeping practices than the profitability of his operation. But it also kept him creating memories, which, from this perspective, were priceless.

My Last Chicken Stew

The last day of the school year at Greenhill school was a time of celebration more commonly referred to as "the chicken stew." My last chicken stew was in 1954, when I graduated from seventh grade.

The event began about 8 a.m. when Dad arrived, gathered firewood with the help of three or four anxious kids, started a roaring fire around a big black cast-iron pot filled with water, and began boiling two old hens. Those hens were as tough as boot heels. The day before, they were running around Mrs. Embry's barnyard, scratching out a living on worms, roots, and the little grain she threw on the ground from time to time. On graduation day, they had the honor of being the main ingredient of the end-of-year celebration. They were boiled a couple of hours before the other ingredients were added, as old hens need the advance heat to make them passably edible. Boiling the other ingredients that long would have made them as mushy as baby food.

People began arriving around nine o'clock—not just students and parents, but the entire Greenhill community. Just about everyone brought something to contribute to the feast. Some brought desserts— chocolate cakes, berry pies, cookies, the good stuff. But most brought ingredients for the stew—either canned or fresh from their garden—tomatoes, corn, potatoes, onions, okra, beans, squash, and just about anything from last year's canning they needed to get rid of before the new season. Dad dumped whatever was offered into the pot with the slowly boiling hens, added liberal amounts of salt and pepper, and stirred the whole mess with a large boat paddle so it wouldn't burn and stick to the bottom and sides of the pot.

At noon, Dad pronounced the stew done and yelled in his loudest voice, "Come and get it! Soup's on. I'm hungry. Let's eat. Gather 'round here for the blessing."

The local Methodist preacher asked the blessing, and Dad ladled big spoons of stew to a long line of hungry people. We sat on the few available chairs and mainly on the ground to enjoy our feast. I ate stew 'till I was filled to the eyelashes and topped it off with a generous sampler of desserts. Most of the others did the same.

When we were unpleasantly full and ready for a siesta, Dad rang the bell and kids slowly gathered in the schoolhouse from all parts of the schoolyard and took their seats. Fifteen first, second, and third graders went to Mrs. Justice's room, and twenty-one students in grades four through seven went into Dad's room. I sat with my seventh-grade classmates, Larry Hall, Sandra Johnson, and Patricia Barnett. Quite a few anxious parents and a few grandparents stood around the edge of the room.

Dad conducted the last class of the year, which was really a simple graduation. Patricia led the group in the "Pledge of Allegiance," and we sang "America the Beautiful." Then Dad handed out report cards and told everyone they had passed to the next grade. He complimented the four of us graduating from seventh grade and wished us the best as we entered town school in Mt. Pleasant the following fall.

The following Saturday, a combined graduation ceremony was held in the Mt. Pleasant High School gym for all the country schools. I was recognized for going the seven years with perfect attendance—and then somewhat embarrassed when another student volunteered that he had also had perfect attendance and wondered why he wasn't recognized. This might have been the only time I received favored treatment because Dad was my teacher and Uncle Paul was the county superintendent. In any case, the graduation was, for some reason, an especially moving experience for me. Since then, I have graduated from school four times, and I don't ever remember being affected as I was that first time.

This was the ending of one phase of my life and the beginning of another. There is an old saying, "You can take a boy out of the country, but you can't take the country out of a boy." This was probably true in my case. The 1954 chicken stew was the beginning of my being taken out of the country, as a couple months later, I entered the town school in Mt. Pleasant, then went off to college, and spent most of my life "out of the country" in the third largest city in the United States. But that country beginning is still in me.

www.ingramcontent.com/pod-product-compliance
Lightning Source LLC
Chambersburg PA
CBHW071740120626
46550CB00002B/593